Life Can't Be All Serious

An Attorney and Magisterial District Judge's Journey through the Lighter Side of Life

By:

William F. Zaun, Esquire

INFINITY PUBLISHING

ISBN 978-0-7414-6051-6

Printed in the United States of America

Published December 2012

INFINITY PUBLISHING

Toll-free (877) BUY BOOK
Local Phone (610) 941-9999
Fax (610) 941-9959
Info@buybooksontheweb.com
www.buybooksontheweb.com

Table of Contents

Dedication

This book is dedicated to my late parents, William S. Zaun and Mae A. Zaun, who worked throughout their lives to provide me with the chance to become a success. This book is also dedicated to my lovely and endearing wife, who has encouraged and supported me in all my endeavors, especially in the writing of this book. She has been and will always be the shining beacon that provides the light to direct our course.

Acknowledgements

I would like to acknowledge the following people who have been instrumental in the preparation and completion of this book: my stepdaughter, Terri Barrall, my loyal and dedicated secretary for over twenty years, who has graciously and painstakingly contributed to the creation of this book; and my stepson, Frank J. Horwath, who not only survived a debilitating stroke in February, 2009, but also recovered through prayers from the whole family with an unmatched dogged determination to provide us with an inspiration to move ahead. I would like to compliment and acknowledge our darling step-granddaughter, Alexis Barrall, who aided and assisted me in the organization of this book.

Finally, I would like to thank my high-school classmate, a trusted friend throughout the years, my golfing partner, and a genuinely respected and accomplished artist, Jim Doddy, for his art design of the cover and illustrations throughout the book.

Rejoice O young man while you are young and let your heart be glad in the days of your youth.

Ecclesiastes 11:9

Grant me a sense of humor, Lord, then saving grace to see a joke, to win some happiness from life, and pass it on to other folks.

Old Irish Blessing

Introduction

For the past thirty-eight years, I have been a practicing attorney and, for the last eight years, a Magisterial District Judge. During that time, there were numerous occasions on which I would meet with other attorneys for coffee or waiting for my case to come up. In those periods of time, we would recount numerous stories from our representations of various clients. I continually received comments from other lawyers, saying, "You really should write a book about some of the people you have encountered and some of the things that have happened to you along the way."

At first, I did not take these requests seriously, but as the years passed by, I began to jot down notes of incidents that I found to be either unusual or comical, or both. When I became a District Judge, I began receiving these comments not only from other lawyers and District Judges but also from police officers, businessmen, and other members of the general public. At some point, I began to take these suggestions seriously and made an initial decision that I would embark on this project, but only after I had retired. My wife thought this would be a good idea probably for dual purposes: (1) I would be doing something gainfully and something I enjoy, and the more probable (2) I would not be sitting idly by on a rocking chair feeding our dog, Max, the maximum amount of his daily intake of food.

What solidified my opinion to proceed with writing this book was attending my fiftieth Bethlehem Catholic High

School reunion. I had only been to one in the past and that was many years ago. At the reunion, my wife and I met up with some fellow graduates, some of which I had not seen in fifty years. I finally found my best and closest friend in high school, Pete, for whom I served as best man at his wedding. He had moved several times — to Ohio, then Texas and Florida — and we, therefore, lost contact with each other. When we sat down for dinner, he started the conversation by saying, "Bill, do you remember the time a couple of us dared you to jump over a parking meter on Webster Street and you not only did not make it but also got hung up on the parking meter?" I purposely did not include this teenage misadventure in the book because it was too humiliating and painful at the time and even more so recounting it now. He went on to mention my unsolicited campaign for high-school class president with my unwanted campaign slogan, "A chicken in every pot," in which I garnered but two votes (a story that is included in this book).

After reliving some other amusing events in which I was involved, I said, "That's it: I am going to write this book." I am hopeful that the following chapters will provide an insight that life as a lawyer or District Judge is a demanding one with some awesome responsibilities because, in some instances, the decisions that you make, in either profession, can affect your clients' liberty or, for people who appear before you, their future life. I always tried to be diligent and mindful of the seriousness of the matters with which I was dealing. On the other hand, as the book title *Life Can't Be All Serious* suggests, humor in good taste and the laughter derived from it truly can be the best medicine. I sincerely wish that the readers of this book will enjoy the sharing of my journey from attorney and District Judge through the lighter side of life.

As a final aside, I wish to mention that throughout this book I have attempted, with very few exceptions, to avoid using real names. Instead, I have created and used fully fictitious names. As Jack Webb used to say in his old show *Dragnet*, "….the names have been changed to protect the innocent."

Chapter One

The Early Years

I was born in February 1942 and was raised by my parents, William S. Zaun and Mae A. Zaun, both now deceased. I am the older of their two children; my sister Barbara Marshall, six years younger, now resides in California. We lived in a working-class neighborhood of West Bethlehem. The first school I attended was St. John Capistrano School (both church and school are now closed by Diocesan consolidation). We were taught by Sisters of Divine Charity and had lunch each school day in the convent basement. My only recollection of any humorous and/or embarrassing events occurred when I served as an altar boy for the first time. The pastor at that time was known as a hard worker for his parish, diligent in his preaching but also known for an occasional outburst of temper. When the first Mass at which I served was over, there was a brief ceremony held afterwards which required me to open the communion rail. After being signaled by the pastor to open the rail, I approached it, pulled it with both hands, but was unable to get it open. Frustrated by my inability to get the rail open, the pastor went to the rail, gave it a hearty kick, and it opened immediately. He then turned to me and, in disgust, said in Hungarian, "Szamar Ember." I had no idea what these words meant, but I knew it could not be anything good.

Later that evening, during our family dinner, my father asked me about my first experience as an altar boy. I told him it went smoothly for the most part until I reached the point of trying to open the communion rail. When I informed him that I was unable to open it and that the pastor turned to me and said, "Szamar Ember," he looked around the table and turned to me with only a slight smile and said, "O my god, Bill, he called you a jackass." I was too young then to predict that it probably would not be the last time that I am called that name.

At the time, both my sister and I were attending grade school, and both my parents were busy operating a poultry stand in the Old City Market at Third and Webster streets on the south side of Bethlehem and another store on Main Street on the north side of Bethlehem. My parents actually met through chickens. My father, along with his father, started a poultry business back in the 1940s where they would sell chickens, geese, ducks, and turkeys at the Allentown Fairgrounds. My mother and her mother, Elmeda Ziegler, had a farm in Breinigsville, and they would transport their poultry to the old Allentown Fairgrounds for sale to customers. Ironically, their poultry stands were located side by side, and as luck and circumstances would have it, they got together, married, and as my father's favorite saying as to how they got married — "we decided to put our eggs into one basket."

Throughout my early years, I was exposed to all types of live poultry — chickens, geese, ducks, guinea hens, and turkeys. I can say honestly, with the benefit of hindsight, that I was not enthralled by the experience. One of my most unpleasant duties was to hand carry the live chicken picked out by the customer as her favorite for the night's dinner, and walk the feathery thing to the room of her eventual demise. Fortunately, I was never called upon to be the actual executioner.

Another of my duties at that time was to deliver poultry orders on Saturdays with an adult driver, since I was too young to drive. We would deliver on an average Saturday at least fifty orders throughout Bethlehem, Hellertown, and Fountain Hill. The route would usually be the same with the first stop being at a notorious watering hole known as the Dew Drop Inn. At that location, the driver known infamously as Louie Lingerer would consistently instruct me that he would make the delivery; all others would be made by me. Invariably, it would always become a long and tedious wait. When he would finally return to the truck, I asked him incredulously, "What took so long?" His answer each time, which I naively accepted, was that the customer could not locate the payment money. So much for youthful ignorance!

During one of the busiest and hectic times of the year, Thanksgiving, while still under the wings of my father and mother, but now old enough to drive, I had numerous orders to deliver to homes on the south side of Bethlehem. With all the flurry of activity, and in a rush to get all the poultry orders delivered, I somehow confused two of the orders. Too much time has passed for me to remember the customers' names but, as an example, I was to deliver a turkey to Mrs. Gobbler on Filmore Street and a goose to Mrs. Feathers on Taylor Street. Inadvertently, I reversed the orders and, as a result, Mrs. Feathers received the turkey, and Mrs. Gobbler, the goose. Within minutes, after each lady had unwrapped their respective orders, they called my father to register their adamant and torrid complaints. As I returned from my route, I distinctly recall my father conveying Mrs. Gobbler's comments to him: "Mr. Zaun, I am totally disgusted and angry about the order that your son delivered to me today. This turkey is the sickest-looking turkey I have ever seen; it has a flat breast and is yellow throughout from its legs to its rear end." Naturally, my father received a similar complaint from Mrs. Feathers stating that she had never seen a goose look like the goose that I had delivered to her. As a result, my father issued a stern reprimand to me, and accordingly, I had to retrieve both birds and deliver them to the right persons.

On another occasion, I was asked by my father to make a delivery to a customer in Fountain Hill. I told him that I could not since I had a baseball practice to attend, but that I could send two of my trusted friends who would make the delivery. They appeared at my father's business. He then gave them directions and gave them change in case the customer would give them a $20 bill. Since the price of the chicken was $6.85, he gave them the wrapped chicken and $13.15 as change. Approximately one hour later, they returned and informed my father that they had made the delivery. Upon asking them for the money paid by the customer, they told him that they had given the customer both the chicken and the $13.15 in change. I am sure the surprised customer did not protest, but as a result, my father told me, in the future, to select friends that are more competent.

Another duty that devolved to me as a son of a poultry business dealer was to hand carry live chickens approximately six blocks to the local rabbi for execution for our Jewish customers. The high school was only one block from the city market, which increased the likelihood that I would be met by one of my high-school classmates on my way to the local rabbi. Most of these trips were uneventful, though on several occasions, some of my classmates would see me and offer taunts such as "there goes the chicken plucker." Reacting to these classmates' insults, I then devised a route through back alleys and side streets that left my hasty travels undetected.

The crowning moment, however, to my experience in working for my parents, came the day of my sophomore year when there was a class election scheduled to be held. Previously, I had been nominated by some still-unknown classmate to be class president. On the day of the election, incidentally, my first and only exposure to the election process at the time, I left my father's business to go to school at 8 a.m. Upon my arrival, to my utter disbelief and consternation, I found that each and every window facing Webster Street, covering at least 15 windows, were signs beautifully and endearingly designed bearing the inscription invoking potential voters to "vote for Bill Zaun, a chicken in every pot." Needless to say, I was totally taken aback, shocked, and now dreadful of what the vote count might be. My best recollection is that there were 38 voting students — with the final vote count 36 for Kline and 2 for Zaun. I remember thinking, *Well, at least I got one vote because I know I voted for myself.* In retrospect, I believe that the vote count was swayed by the vegetarian element in my class.

Chapter Two

The Learning Years

In 1955, I enrolled in the freshman class at the original Bethlehem Catholic High School, which was located on Fourth and Webster streets on the south side of Bethlehem or, as one of the lines of the school's alma mater states, "amid Bethlehem's verdant hills." There was a faculty of about three priests and twelve nuns. The nuns were sincere in their attitude, dedicated to teaching, and ultra stern in administering discipline.

One of the nuns, who I will identify as Sister Forgetful, taught English and usually was the last class of the day. On one particular rainy day, she taught us her English class, and as the time for dismissal approached, she realized that she could not locate her "rubbers," i.e. the protection gear worn over shoes on rainy, wet days. As the minutes ticked by and out of frustration by not finding her rubbers, she announced to the class that we would all stay for as long as it took until the culprit would admit to stealing the rubbers. No one spoke up, though there were whispers of discontent among the students who were anxious to leave and go home. Sister Forgetful, as did all the other nuns, wore habits that were floor length, making it difficult to see their shoes. An hour and a half later, after more warnings of impending punishment for the thief, one of the students in the first row spoke up and said, "Sister, I think you are wearing your rubbers." She immediately tucked on her habit and saw that, indeed, she was wearing the alleged and suspected, stolen rubbers. Her only comment was "Class is dismissed."

Back in the late '50s, possession of tobacco products, and certainly use of them in our high school, was strictly prohibited. On several occasions, I can remember assemblies being held for pat-down searches of suspected students who had cigarettes usually hidden in their socks. On one occasion, four male students entered the boys' room ostensibly to relieve themselves but also for the purpose of smoking a cigarette. As all four were standing at their individual urinals, they began passing the cigarette to each other. Suddenly and unannounced, Sister Search and Seizure burst into the room and said, "Master Johnson, what do you have in your hand?" I can only tell you that his response did not include or refer to any cigarettes.

Each year our school would have an extracurricular activity such as participation in an operetta or play. One of the plays was the well-known show *Oklahoma*. One of the intractable rules was that each person who was selected for a part had to attend each scheduled practice held after school hours. A missed, unexcused absence from practice meant you were out of the show. At the end of the auditions, I was selected to play the part of a cowboy, "Slim." I am sure that my selection had more to do with my physical build than it did my acting ability. In any event, I attended each and every practice, I believe, thirty in number. Finally, on the night the show was presented to the public for the first time, I had the chance to deliver my one line: "Did you get the wagons hitched yet?" I was able to deliver my one line without a hitch and without applause.

On the second night of this same show, we were all dressed up as cowboys and were placed by Sister No-Nonsense on the steps adjacent to the stage waiting for our turn to make our entrance. While sitting on the steps, one of the students, Bob Impulsive, known for being outspoken and many times out of place, raised his hand and asked Sister No-Nonsense if he could use the bathroom. Her answer was curt and emphatic, "No, you may not; we are going onstage in three minutes." To which Bob instantaneously and just as emphatically responded, "All right, I'll piss in my hat." Such a crude retort in a Catholic high school in 1958 simply would not be tolerated, and accordingly, Bob was the recipient of a swift left jab and right uppercut that silenced us all.

My recollection of classes in high school is that cheating on tests was not prevalent but, on occasion, did occur. One example that remains firmly embedded in my memory because of its uniqueness occurred in biology class my sophomore year. The nun in charge handed out a biology test that required twenty answers. I had contemplated for some time the answer to question #8 but could not come up with an answer. For some inexplicable reason, I wrote next to #8, "I don't know the answer." Sitting directly across from me was a fellow male student, Joe Rubberneck, who I saw several times peering over at my paper. When the test was over and all papers handed in, the nun-teacher said she would have the test results the following day. On the next day during biology class, the nun called Joe up to the front of the class and accused him of cheating. His admission of guilt came quickly when the teacher showed him my paper and then his answer, which contained at #8 the blatant incriminatory answer, "I don't know the answer either."

I have already alluded to several incidents in which the nuns, who taught us back in the late fifties, exhibited a penchant for strict compliance with the rules and discipline for violation of those rules. The atmosphere for their teachings was serious and austere. On the other hand, to their credit, they instilled in their students the need to show respect for those in authority and to treat others as you would want to be treated. Most importantly, they succeeded in setting forth certain moral values that would act as invaluable guidelines for all of us no matter what career or job path we eventually chose.

As the following story will show, they were not without their own innate sense of humor. When I was a junior in high school, I was taught geometry by Sister Perseverance. It certainly was not my favorite subject, and I am positive that I was not her favorite student. I recall, in fact, her stating that I could not even draw a straight line and that the likelihood of me ever being able to do so was minimal. At that time, I believed her to be one of the oldest members of the faculty and estimated her age as being in the seventies. Approximately twenty-six years later, my oldest daughter, Sharon, attended and then graduated from Bethlehem Catholic High School. While she was still attending school, I went to pick her up after school, and as I parked my car near to the door she would exit, I looked out the car window and saw Sister Perseverance. I thought surely my eyesight must be deteriorating rapidly, but as I approached her, I knew that it was not a mirage. She greeted me warmly, although she did comment that I had not parked my car straight and completely parallel to the sidewalk. The first words out of my mouth were "Sister, after all these years, you look great!" Without a moment's hesitation, she said in response, "That's because I use oil of delay."

During my grade-school and high-school years, I was an avid fan and follower of major sports: football, basketball, and baseball. Fondly, I recall at a young age, attending Liberty High School football games with my father, memorizing uniform numbers and game statistics. While in high school, one Liberty High School game stands out in my memory and not because of the final score. My father and I and another stand owner in the city market, Jim Proudfather, went to the football game. Jim came wearing a heavy overcoat with a large inside pocket, inside which was a large flask containing his favorite beverage, Jack Daniel's. He was not only an ardent fan but an emotional one too because he had two sons on the team. In the first half, his oldest son, Luke, reeled off three lengthy touchdown runs zigzagging through the opposition with the ease of young Jim Thorpe. As his son was running for the goal line, he would push, as if helping his son, those next to him at least a few inches down the row. As his son scored the first touchdown, he took a long swig from his flask, jumped up, fist held high in the air, and shouted, "That's my boy! That's my boy!" He repeated these same motions and shouts each time his son scored his three touchdowns in the first half. Soon after the second half began, the coach inserted Jim's other son into the lineup. Sure enough, as luck would have it, he returned the second half kickoff from his own two-yard line and ran in dazzling fashion for a ninety-eight yard touchdown. Jim, by now full of pride, and Jack Daniel's, took another long swig from his flask and this time, with both fists raised high in the air, jumped up and hollered, "That's my other boy! That's my other boy!" Sitting next to Jim was a tall, thin, reserved gentleman who sat quietly through most of the game. Now, with his ribs probably bruised by Jim's thrusting elbows and near deaf from his repeated bellowing outbursts, he stood up, faced Jim directly, and demandingly asked, "Just how many bleeping sons do you have?" I don't remember Jim's answer but I do recall the rows of laughter that ensued.

During my childhood years, I loved to follow sports, but I had never played basketball, other than in neighborhood pickup games. By my third year, knowing that I had virtually no chance to make the starting team, but hopeful that I could still make the team, I decided to try out for the high-school basketball team. The first tryout was scheduled for a weekday night. I showed up along with about twenty other hopefuls. The coach initially put us through some running and dribbling drills. He then put us through a rather common drill where two lines are formed facing the basket. The first person in line 1 dribbles to the basket and shoots as the first person in line 2 goes in to get the rebound and passes the ball to the second person in line 1, who then drives to the basket. I happened to be in line 2, ran in to get the rebound, and then rather forcefully (probably trying to impress the coach with my passing prowess) passed the ball to the next person in line 1. That person just happened to be the high scorer from the past year and was considered to be the most valuable player on the team. Unfortunately, when I threw the ball, it caught him directly in the ribs and he fell to the ground writhing in pain. After checking out his star player, the coach lectured me about the thrust of my pass. It did not take long for me to find out my fate for the next day: my name was scratched off the tryout list.

My only other attempt to participate in high-school athletics came when, again in my third year of high school, I decided to try out for the baseball team. At least, this time, I did have some experience since in grade school I played Little League baseball and then later in a CYO league. After a couple of tryouts, I found out that I had made the team as a reserve third baseman. My expectations were that I would see some action, maybe in the late innings. Four games into the season, without a grass stain on my uniform, the coach finally called me to pinch-hit. I got a walk and was now looking at the coach for a possible steal sign, which I believe was him touching his hat. I saw him nip at his hat and off I went and made it to second, except in doing so, when I slid, my cleats went into the opposing second baseman just above his shins and I could see that the contact caused bleeding. The opposing coach was irritated and upset and began ranting about hurting his player. I did not feel better when I saw an ambulance pull up and take him to the hospital. Several innings later, a teammate (who I should have known was a prankster) told me, "Bill, you better start praying; I just heard he's in pretty bad shape." Knowing his injury was just a cut, I found his comment hard to believe, yet I was rattled by it. Thankfully, after nervously sweating, my teammate admitted that he had made up the story. Later, I found out that he was fine and had taken about seven stitches at the hospital.

Three games later, I had not made any appearances and began wondering whether I would just spend the rest of the season gathering splinters by riding the bench. One game later, the coach relented and put me in the game as a pinch runner. I ran out to second base and was told beforehand that the steal sign was any contact by the coach to his forehead. I looked at the coach intently, but his hands never made it above his waist. No steal sign was given, and I guess my thinking was *The hell with it — I may not get into another game. I might as well go out with a blaze of glory.* On the next pitch, I took off for third base — was out by ten feet, if not more. To make matters worse, in sliding, I ripped the one pant leg completely and the coach was soon standing over me, saying, "OK Zaun, back to the bench" as he held his hand on his forehead. Since I had gone out in a blaze of dust instead of a blaze of glory, he might as well have said, "OK Zaun, back to the bus and don't come back."

I graduated from high school in June 1959 with no other distinction or adulation other than the notation, under my high-school yearbook picture, "distinguished dresser bound for Georgetown."

Chapter Three

Summer Job Interludes

After my junior year in high school, I worked for the next four summers on two different golf courses from June to September. The initial rate of pay was $1.10 an hour before taxes. My job responsibilities included weeding and raking sand traps, fertilizing and mowing greens, and other overall maintenance jobs. When I first started, the place we reported to work, where we had coffee breaks and ate lunch, was a tiny shack with a sofa, a table, and a couple of chairs. I distinctly remember that you could not ascertain the color of the walls because they were covered from floor to ceiling with Playmates of the Month that must have covered the entire past decade. Because of this décor, since my mother drove me to work and picked me up, I always made certain that I was dropped off far from the shack and picked up outside the shack.

Our boss was a very tall man, who I swear wore a size-17 shoe, and was kindhearted and understanding. Our foreman was also outgoing and had a sincere demeanor. On one unforgettable occasion, the superintendent, who lived about two blocks from the maintenance shack and directly next to the outskirts of the golf course, asked our foreman if he could please spray his lawn and rosebushes surrounding his home to enhance its appearance. For spraying greens, we used a mixture that would not only nurture the grass but also would make its appearance a lush green. For spraying sand traps that would be filled with weeds, we used a substance that could eradicate any type of plant. In responding to the request, our foreman dutifully went out to the garage and filled the 500 or so gallon spraying dispenser tank. But he unintentionally and unknowingly used the wrong mixture — not the green grass enhancer but the weed eliminator and eradicator. He proceeded to the superintendent's home and sprayed the entire lawn: front yard, back yard, side yards, and made sure to spray the rosebushes that adorned and enveloped the entire home. About eighteen hours later, as I was driving to work and passing the home lawn sprayed the previous day, I had to stop and look. Did part of the Sahara desert suddenly appear in Bethlehem? Yes, it did. The entire lawn was desolate of any color; the rosebushes sagged in sadness and truly looked like the last roses of summer. As I remember, the foreman sheepishly apologized for his mistake. The lawn would not return to any semblance of a lush green until at least the following year. My own adage to this unfortunate saga would be as follows: "Be wary of what you have sprayed, for you may very easily be betrayed and dismayed."

The second memorable event that I personally witnessed while working on the golf course was of a totally different nature. One bright and beautiful summer morning, I was out at 8 a.m. cutting one of the eighteen greens on the course. It would be our practice before the morning to see if any golfers were about to hit on the green and, if so, would wait until they had completed the hole and then resume the mowing. As I saw the foursome on the tee, I waved them on and stood by as they hit their balls. What took place next shocked me to the core. Of the foursome, two players stood off the green, one was on the green, and one in the sand trap. Incomprehensibly, the player in the sand trap swung at his ball, which flew out of the trap, striking his partner on the side of the head with a sickening thud. The struck player fell to the ground instantly and appeared to be unconscious and unresponsive. An ambulance was summoned, arrived, and took him to the hospital. None of us received a word as to his condition. At about 3:30 p.m., I was about to mow the last green for the day, when I was astounded to see the same gentleman, who had been struck in the morning, not only back on the golf course but also finishing the final nine holes. I was told later that he was unconscious until he reached the hospital, then regained consciousness, had x-rays taken, which were negative, and decided to return to finish his round. Up to that point, I thought I had seen everything possible on the golf course but this incident topped them all.

My final summer of working at a golf course occurred between my college years. Ironically, a new course was being built under the auspices of my old boss. He graciously hired me and assigned me to my first task — delivering eight glass water bottles throughout the course. I loaded all the containers on the Jeep, and then he asked me, "Bill, are you sure you know how to drive stick shift?" In the past, I believe, I had driven a stick shift one time for a brief period of time. Somewhat unsure of my ability to drive the Jeep but wanting to keep the new job, I said, "Sure."

I started the Jeep with my boss standing by, popped the clutch, and instantaneously, as if on cue, all eight containers fell off the Jeep and shattered completely. Red faced and wondering why I didn't say, "No," he responded with unexpected grace by responding, "Bill, from now on you are limited to hoofing it or using a golf cart at best." After completing my last summer on the links, I was happy to return to my educational pursuits.

Chapter Four

The Enlightening Years

After graduating from high school, I applied to and was accepted by Georgetown University in Washington, D.C., which was approximately 200 miles away from my home in Bethlehem, Pennsylvania. Upon my arrival, I experienced the usual and normal freshman anxieties. I was quite frankly homesick, somewhat forlorn, and wondering what my future might hold. In this atmosphere, I tried by all my means to do my best but found that after the first semester that my grade-point average could endanger my staying in school. At this time, I was visited by my parents, expressed my frustration, felt inconsolable, and told them I was ready to call it quits. Without hesitation, my father gave me a conclusive and momentous choice, which I would describe as a defining moment in my life. The proposition that still rings in my ears, "Bill, you can leave now or stay, but if you leave now you are coming home to kill chickens." The mere thought of this dire possibility caused me to stay in school, work harder with more resolve, and actually catapulted me through Georgetown University.

Reflecting on my years at Georgetown, I conjure up memories of hard, studious work with an intense desire to succeed, but this college experience was not without its lighter moments.

In my freshman year, 1959, hazing on campus was still in vogue. Because of some of the more outrageous hazing ordeals, the university outlawed this sometimes-insidious practice the following year. My recollection of what I was subjected to was wearing a silly-looking beanie, which, of course, had to be worn backwards, rolling up your pant legs to your knees and, finally, placing your tie in your mouth. These crazy outfits were the "order of the day," while walking to class for the first week of school. Since some of the classes were held a block off campus, the hazed and dazed freshmen would have to endure the not-so-flattering whistles from busloads of students who would pass by on their way to school. In order to suppress any freshmen uprising, the sophomore class would round up any suspected leaders of the movement. Each such selected person would have their heads ignominiously shaved, with the word "leader" emblazoned on their shaved heads. Thankfully, the hazing period was not of long duration and we were now able to focus our efforts towards studying for classes and tests.

One diversion from the classroom routine was an event held annually in which students would attend a weekend retreat in the hills of rural Virginia. A retreat is designed to provide students with a time for prayer, silent reflection, and introspection. We were told in advance that talking throughout the weekend would not be permitted, except in a case of emergency. One especially innovative person, Reginald Retreatless, was determined to prepare himself for this institutionally imposed aura of silence. His father happened to be a licensed physician in Vermont and Reginald was somehow able to obtain a hypodermic needle. He proceeded to buy a dozen and a half oranges and a quart of vodka, which he injected into the oranges and loaded them into his suitcase to be taken to the retreat. As we arrived at the old and quaint retreat house, we were ushered into various rooms, all of which contained signs in Latin with the inscription "Maxima Silentium," meaning maximum silence. I do not recall any violations of this directive and even Reginald, despite his diet of his treasured oranges, was able to maintain his silence although he did so with a devious smile on his face.

In my sophomore year, I was assigned to a dormitory that was connected to and immediately adjacent to the Georgetown University Hospital and the nursing center. I can remember vividly many of the premed students led by a student known as Tom Peeping, who incidentally is now a well-regarded cardiologist in California, climbing up to the roof of the dormitory armed with high-powered binoculars, in hopes of capturing a view of some of the all-female nursing students. Their efforts were unsuccessful probably because the nursing students were forewarned to keep their blinds closed.

During the same year, the university had planned a state-of-the-art science building. The groundbreaking was scheduled, and dignitaries from the diplomatic corps, local politicians, senators, and representatives were invited to attend. The guest speaker was Bob Hope, the well-known top comedian of this time. Somehow, a few of the premed students learned of the impending groundbreaking ceremony and the area in which it was to be held. They then managed to hatch a plot that they perceived, if successful, would lead to a historic comic moment. The night before the ceremony, under the cover of darkness, which may now, in retrospect, be considered as a mini precursor of Watergate, several students, flashlights in hand, approached the cordoned-off section where the groundbreaking was to take place. They proceeded to dig up the area, filled the hole with loads of empty beer cans, and then neatly covered the beer-can cache with dirt. The next morning, which I recall, was a bright and beautiful sunny day; the dignitaries arrived along with the university president to conduct the ceremony. The president of the university presented Bob Hope with a special gold-embossed shovel and invited him to break the ground symbolizing the beginning of a new science building. Much to the astonishment and chagrin of the university president, Mr. Hope proceeded to dig the shovel into the ground and came up with beer cans instead of dirt. As best as I can recall, Bob Hope was able to make light of the quite embarrassing moment with one of his patented and colorful off-the-cuff jokes. I know that an investigation of the plot was commenced, but to my knowledge, none of the perpetrators were ever identified.

During my years at Georgetown, football was only an intramural sport and the basketball team had not yet managed to become a nationally ranked and powerhouse team. In my junior year, we played Lafayette at home in a packed, noisy, and hot McDonough Gymnasium on campus. During the game, one could see that there was a lot of tension between the opposing guards, with heated words being exchanged between them on almost every possession. Shortly thereafter, a fight broke out between the two players; the respective benches emptied and fans left the stands to join the ugly fray. It was truly an all-out brawl, the likes of which I had never seen either in person or on television. Unfortunately, one of the most good-hearted Jesuit priests, Father B., ran onto the gym floor hoping to stave off and diffuse the now-near riot. He tapped on the shoulder of our six-foot nine-inch center who must have thought that it was a probable Lafayette attacker. The Georgetown player instinctively turned around and simultaneously swung, breaking the peacemaker priest's nose.

As the fighting worsened and with no end in sight, the few campus police present tried their best to quell the outbreak, to no avail. Meanwhile, in the public address announcer's booth, someone came up with the idea to play the national anthem in hopes that this would awaken the combatants' patriotic spirit and return them to reason. The chief public address announcer, who just happened to be a Bethlehem native, flustered by all the turmoil on the court, grabbed the 78 RPM record, which contained "The Star-Spangled Banner" and nervously proceeded to drop the record leaving it in pieces and unusable. Fortunately, for all involved, the District of Columbia police soon arrived and were able to restore law and order.

For my first three years, I lived on campus in a college dorm. In those years, each floor had an assigned Jesuit priest to serve as that floor's prefect. This priest would attempt to ensure that the students were orderly and acting properly. In my sophomore year, I lived in a four-story dorm, each floor having an assigned Jesuit prefect. It was common practice for the priest on our floor to hang his cassock on the outside of his door for pickup by the drycleaners that served our campus. One of the more imaginative and conniving students on our floor was Steve Lifter. For weeks, he kept notes of the times that the priest would hang out his cassock and the times when it would be picked up by the drycleaner. One day, he decided the time had come for him to make his move. He grabbed the cassock, changed clothes, and donned the priest's cassock. He then, unabashedly and brazenly, walked the approximate seven blocks to Wisconsin Avenue and entered the liquor store. He spoke to the store clerk and then ordered six bottles of the best Scotch the store had in stock, and told the clerk that he should bill the Jesuit community located on campus. Without concern, he strolled back to the campus and stashed away the fruits of his crime. To my knowledge, no one was ever able to identify the culprit and he went undetected, although I do believe that he never again attempted this stunt.

In June 1963, I graduated from Georgetown University with an A.B. degree in government and began preparing for the LSAT exam in anticipation of applying to Villanova Law School.

Chapter Five

The Years of Advocacy Training

At some point in my junior year at Georgetown, I decided to go to law school, influenced in great part by an elderly, astute professor who taught a course entitled "Law and the Laws." A cousin of mine introduced me to another prospective Villanova law student, and we immediately embarked on finding suitable housing for our next three years at law school. With pure luck on our side, we answered an ad in a local newspaper and were accepted by the landlord-widow to rent a third-floor apartment at the unbelievable price of $28 a month, including utilities. She happened to be more concerned with living all alone than with the price of rent. We were happy to accommodate and soon went out and purchased an old refrigerator somewhat similar to the one seen on Jackie Gleason's *The Honeymooners*. The total cost was $15. In addition, we bought a hot plate for $7. We now felt we were on our way to pursue the study of law. My roommate was one of a kind: constantly upbeat, always joking with a constant view towards the brighter side of life. His father was a well-respected rectal surgeon who he would jokingly refer to as the "Rear Admiral." When people would inquire how his dad was doing in his profession, he would always answer by saying, "My dad's business is always looking up." If I would ask him a question with a somewhat obvious answer, he would usually reply, "Bill, is the Pope Protestant? Does a bear s--- in the woods? Is the moon made of blue cheese?" I will make mention of him later for his propensity to play jokes on people, in one instance on me.

On the very first day of law school, we were addressed by the Law School Dean, who is now deceased, who was well respected and revered by both the faculty and the student body. His very first comment to the first-year class was prophetic and probably heard in other institutions of higher learning: "Ladies and Gentlemen, look to your right and left of you. Chances are excellent that after three years here, you will not see one or both of them." He reminded us that located across the street from the law school was an Augustinian seminary and that if we wanted justice, we should cross the street, but if we wanted money, we should stay at the law school. His admonitions and prognostications proved to be quite true. No one crossed the street to enter the seminary, and by the end of my third year at the law school, the class *was* cut in half.

Law school, as I remember it, was pretty much nose to the grindstone, hours and hours of study, hours of class preparation, and a need to be on your toes when called upon to argue your position. If you were truly serious about succeeding, then there was little opportunity for partying and idle time.

However, I can now recall at least two instances during law school that were cause for laughter. In the second year of law school, we were called upon to participate in a moot court competition, which continues to this very day. Two law school students were paired to compete against two others. The judges were volunteers, mostly successful lawyers who were law-school alumni. I was paired with a very competent and knowledgeable student, known as Benny Contrite, as I will now refer to him. After months of preparation, the time came for us to argue our positions before the panel of moot court judges. Benny Contrite was called upon first, and for some inexplicable reason, he just totally froze and was simply too unnerved to talk. That gave us a beginning score of zero. Needless to say, this made the task of winning impossible. It was similar to your opponent in bowling rolling two consecutive three hundred games and your team rolling ten straight gutter balls. I have recently learned that my partner on that day is a now quite successful lawyer. His baptismal fire that day certainly led him on to greater accomplishments.

One moment during law school that remains forever imbedded on my psyche and memory was an innocent Saturday morning, when I was experiencing car trouble with my old Ford. Cars were never and still are not my forte. Their inner workings were totally foreign to me. In fact, turning the key and hearing the engine rev were enough to satisfy me. On the other hand, my roommate, Ed Easy, who was the only person on earth who called me Willie, was knowledgeable and proficient with car mechanics. On this particular Saturday morning, I informed him of the problems I was having with my old Ford. He graciously agreed to take a look at the car to see if he could diagnose the cause. He put on his overalls and went outside to begin his search for the problem. At least one hour later, he came up the stairs in oil-soaked overalls and gleefully told me that he had found the source of the malfunction. He said that my old Ford had a broken knibbly pin, which could easily and quickly be repaired. He further suggested that I take the car to the Exxon gas station on Lancaster Avenue and to ask to see the head mechanic. Trusting in his advice and happy that my car would once again be running smoothly, I went directly to the gas station and asked to see the head mechanic. I told him my car had a broken knibbly pin and asked if he could have it repaired. To this day, I vividly remember, at first, the incredulous look on his face and then the ensuing, voluminous laughter by him and his gathering fellow mechanics. I knew then that I had been had and promised myself never again to be so naïve and ignorant about vehicle parts and vehicle repair.

Chapter Six

The Years of Discipline

After receiving my law degree from Villanova Law School, I embarked on the next necessary step: preparing for the Pennsylvania Bar Exam. This period of time coincided with the middle of the Vietnam War years, and I was subject to the draft because I finished law school, therefore ending my deferment. I was fortunate enough to enlist in the Pennsylvania National Guard unit in Easton, Pennsylvania, and soon found myself on my way to Fort Jackson in Columbia, South Carolina, for basic training. The mode of transportation to basic training was by train (more like a cattle car) from Harrisburg, Pennsylvania. After a twenty-six-hour bouncy and very uncomfortable ride, we found ourselves close to the entrance to Fort Jackson. Nearby the Fort were two restaurants both having "Whites Only" signs in their windows. I had never entertained a bias or prejudice towards blacks, so those signs came as a total shock to me. After disembarking from the train, we were directed to run up a long, steep hill aptly named "Drag Ass Hill" with full and heavy duffle bag in hand. It was then that I realized how out of shape I was and how the forthcoming training would be difficult for me. I quickly became aware that I was a twenty-five-year-old amongst eighteen-year-old enlistees and draftees. In any case, after reaching the barracks area, aching and out of breath, we were greeted by a not so friendly, tall, and imposing black drill sergeant who was about to announce the first assignment, KP. He barked out that the first assignment would be in alphabetical order. I breathed a sigh of relief since being last was not all foreign to me. Minutes later, I knew that this must be a sign of things to come when the drill sergeant announced that KP would commence in reverse alphabetical order. Naturally, I was first in line. We reported to the mess hall at 6:00 p.m. and stayed through until 2:00 a.m., at which time a sergeant inspected the hundreds of trays that we had washed and cleaned. He claimed that he had found a piece of lint on one tray and, therefore, we would be required to redo each and every tray. We finally finished at 4:30 a.m. with an impending wake-up call at 5:30 a.m. Upon reaching my barracks totally exhausted, I remember falling onto the bunk bed in full uniform, boots and all, and falling asleep within seconds.

Also, in the first week of training, we were asked to fill out a questionnaire including our educational background. I purposely omitted law school (which, in retrospect, was a big mistake), thinking that I would receive more stringent treatment if this fact were known to the drill sergeant. Well, the omission did not last very long, as one of the sergeant instructors, the most imposing and physically impressive one, called me out to go to the drill field with him. Upon reaching the field, he put me through the manual of arms with the M-16 in rapid, demanding staccato fashion. His loud, barking commands — "Right Shoulder Arms," "Left Shoulder Arms," "Port Arms" — had me totally unraveled, confused to the point I did not know my right from my left. After making several mistakes, he finally said to me, "Son, are you sure you went to law school? Did you get your degree in the mail?" His message sunk in, and I painfully realized the benefits of full disclosure.

There were three other occasions when I was in the military that confirmed that I was not destined to be an Audie Murphy and that I was more akin, if I must say so, to Beetle Bailey of old comic-page notoriety.

While at Fort Indiantown Gap near Harrisburg, Pennsylvania, for our annual summer training, we were told that on the next morning, we would be inspected by a visiting two-star general. The inspection was to take place in our barracks with each soldier in full uniform standing at his respective bunk. On the bunk bed, we were told to display all our personal items and equipment. To this day, I am convinced that I was set up by some of my fellow soldiers. About an hour before the time of the inspection, I could not locate my left low quarter dress shoe and had only the right shoe. After frantically looking in each nook and cranny of the barracks and asking for assistance from my fellow platoon members, I was finally approached by one of my friends, Joe Totheresue, who told me that he had found a low quarter shoe but that it was a right-footed shoe. I now had two shoes, but both right-footed, I decided that I had no other alternative but to somehow put on both shoes and get ready for the inspection. The experience was excruciating and humiliating, and I was left wondering how long, if at all, that I could stand with two right shoes on my feet. More importantly, I was concerned that if the General noticed it, what would the punishment be for such a violation? Sure enough, the inspecting General entered the barracks and came up to me within inches of my face and looked at me up and down. After asking my name, he walked around my bunk, peering at all the items on my bunk bed. I stood there, my heart beating incessantly, when with a stern expression and baritone voice he said, "Soldier, do you realize that your fork is missing from your mess kit?" Fortunately, this omission was considered a minor infraction or as we would refer to it in the law as being de minimus. My only punishment was the pain in my left foot, which endured for a couple of days.

After basic training, I was sent for advanced training at Fort Gordon near Augusta, Georgia. Somehow, in a minor way, my law-school training had an impact as I was assigned to the Special Services unit that was in charge of entertainment for the base. My immediate supervisor was a Major who had a particular liking for Wild Turkey (not the flying fowl variety).

On one particular weekend evening, I was just relaxing on my bunk reading a book when a staff sergeant, a native of

Guam, came in abruptly and said to me, "I am placing you on cannon duty tomorrow because a four-star General is visiting and will be inspecting the troops after the arrival ceremony." *Cannon duty? Cannon duty?* I thought maybe I was dreaming and I was somehow in the Revolutionary War. It seemed odd that I had received such short notice, although our barracks was immediately adjacent to Headquarters Company where the base commander resided and where the ceremony would be held. I had fired an M-16 many times but had never been close to a cannon except at a college football game. We were told that our uniform had to be in A1 shape. Since all of my available green fatigue shirts were wrinkled or dirty or both, I spent the next few hours asking any other non-duty soldiers in my barracks if I could borrow theirs. Finally, one supportive soldier said I could use his. It was clean, heavily starched, and in ten times better shape than my own. The only problem was that his nametag sewn on the fatigue shirt bore his unbelievably long name, something like GREENSCHLAGEN. I thanked him profusely and wore his uniform the next day.

We had a relatively short practice firing the cannons, and much to my surprise, it was not that difficult. On the day of the actual ceremony, six cannons were aligned for firing, with each cannon having a two-man team, one to load and one to fire. Much to my amazement, all the cannons functioned properly. However, it was now time for the General to inspect the troops fronting each of the fired cannons. As the General with precision steps approached us, I figured my odds for not being inspected were pretty good: one in twelve, decent Vegas odds. Lo and behold, the General with military precision marched past the first four cannons and then did an abrupt right face, right to my position. My mind at that moment was agog and increasingly wary of any questions the General might ask me. He said rather kindly, "Son, what's your name?" I tried to say it without hesitation. "Greenschlagen, Sir." He then asked me where I was from and, luckily, I remembered that the person who gave me his shirt was from Greenwich, Connecticut. I thought any more questions and I'll have to be creative or else I'll be toast. In rapid succession, I asked myself, *I wonder how many bridges are in Greenwich. I wonder if there is a North and a South Greenwich.* As I pondered these possible questions, the General asked me, "Do you get a lot of snow up there?" I quickly responded, "Tons of it, Sir." He simply said, "Very good, carry on." With a sigh of relief, I promised myself I would never borrow clothing from anyone again.

After completing advanced training at Fort Gordon, I returned to my home unit in Easton for the remaining term of my six-year enlistment. At some point, another Guardsman and I became interested in becoming officers and were sent to Fort Indiantown Gap for the initial training weekend. Upon arrival, we were placed in platoons and barracks in alphabetical order. This sequence, by now, was becoming old hat for me. The net result, however, was that each platoon would have to start running one-half hour before breakfast, lunch, and dinner. Being in the last platoon meant we ran for what seemed like forever and dead last.

On the second day of training, I was approached by a TAC officer who said that he wanted to inspect my uniform. This procedure was likewise becoming old hat for me. He proceeded to ask me what was wrong with my uniform. As he asked, he began tugging on some of my chest hairs. I went through my mental checklist, starting with "my boots are not polished, my hair is too long, my brass is not polished." With each unsatisfactory answer, the TAC officer would increase the tugging to the point that it was becoming quite intimidating. Throughout this whole process, I did not sense any relationship between his tugging motions and my uniform. I continued to rattle off answers that by now were complete guesses. "My shirt is not properly starched. I don't have a straight gig line." His answer continued to be "wrong," and I sensed that he was becoming weary of my answers and I knew that I was just about devoid of any chest hair. Finally, he said that I was wearing the wrong T-shirt, which was V-necked and not army regulation at the time. The persistent non-stop running and chest-hair pulling, along with eating meals in West Point fashion with only a few minutes to eat, convinced me that this was not to be my calling in life. My friend and I left after that weekend and returned to our regular positions with our unit in Easton.

Original Zaun's Poultry Market in southside Bethlehem with the owners, my grandfather, Frank Zaun and my grandmother, Elizabeth Zaun, circa 1940.

My father, William S. Zaun and mother, Mae A Zaun with me.

My sister Barbara and I

My first encounter with poultry.

High School picture with old friend Pete.

Swearing in by Judge Grifo as an Attorney.

Swearing in by Judge Freedberg as a Magisterial District Justice, with my wife Til. Judge Jack Panella, top right.

At Magisterial District Justice bench with my wife Til.

My stepdaughter , Terri with her children Ashley, Eric and Alexis.

Til and myself.

My stepson Frank with his wife , Stacey and their daughters, Alyssa and Kaelah.

Chapter Seven

The Years of Advocacy

After completing my military service with the Pennsylvania National Guard, I prepared for the Pennsylvania Bar Exam and took the test in Pittsburgh, Pennsylvania. Upon learning that I had passed the exam, I began the private practice of law on Main Street in downtown Bethlehem.

One of the first clients that I had was a middle-aged woman who came to my office without an appointment. Curious as to how she chose to see me, she said that she looked at the four attorney names on the façade of the building and liked my name the best. Although I considered this less than a ringing endorsement, I was quite happy to see how she might need my legal services. She explained that she would like me to prepare her Last Will and Testament. I then went through all the usual considerations in preparing to make a will, along with some suggestions. She was agreeable to the terms, and I told her to give me a week or two to have the will ready for her signature. She then said that she had one request that she had omitted in our conversation. After I asked her the nature of the omission, she, in a normal tone of voice, said that, upon her death, she would like to have her remains wrapped in pure silk and flown for burial next to the tomb of King Farouk. A bit taken aback but still indulging, I told her, in a kindly manner, that this was a rather bizarre request, which I could not accommodate in her will. She insisted, emphatically, that this term must be included, and if it was not, she did not want me to prepare her will. Sadly, I informed her that this provision raised a question of competency and felt it improper to prepare her will under these terms. She left the office abruptly, mumbling that she would seek out another lawyer who would be more understanding and who would include her burial provision.

A few months later, somewhat settled in my Main Street office, a middle-aged couple made an appointment to see me to have their will prepared. A few weeks prior, in fact on my birthday, my parents purchased a high-back leather judge's chair for me to use in my office. The couple came in promptly in the morning, and I spent about forty-five minutes with them discussing the details of their wills. I informed them that I would call them when their wills were ready, explained my fee, and told them I would see them again within ten days. Just a few moments after they departed, I leaned back on my new chair, probably thinking about the next upcoming appointment, when suddenly and without warning, the large spring attached to the back of the chair sprung and the force of its snapping, literally, catapulted me in the air. I landed face down on the floor with part of the chair now lying on top of me. The other attorneys and secretaries, on hearing the loud noise and commotion, came rushing to my assistance and asked if I was injured. As I recall, I told them that I was not hurt but that my pride was certainly wounded. My very first thought, however, was thinking about the possible reaction of my clients had they been present when I became the Flying Wallenda. Needless to say, I replaced the chair and had no further incidents with it.

On one particularly hot July day in the 1970s, I was scheduled to appear in court in Easton for an ARD hearing. These hearings are usually held to confirm or deny ARD (a program for first-time offenders), usually heavily attended, and are held en masse. For some reason, I was delayed leaving my office and knew that I would be a little late for the hearing. I just happened to be wearing a brand-new suit, which I had purchased a week before. As I recall, it was an extremely hot and muggy day, so I decided to take off my coat and placed it over the passenger seat of my car. The air conditioning on my car was not working, and in hindsight, I opened the car windows to alleviate the heat in the car. Route 22 was always my chosen route to the courthouse, since it was the shortest and easiest way to get there. As I was within a few miles of Easton, the force of the wind coming through the window threw my suit coat out the window. I immediately looked in my rear-view mirror and could see a tractor-trailer speedily going over my coat. Not being the type of person to easily give up losing a brand-new suit coat, I pulled over to the shoulder of the road and after looking for it for a few minutes found it a couple of feet from the guardrail laying in a torn and tattered condition in the weeds. Knowing that it was now too late to return to my office for another coat, I proceeded to the courthouse more worried about appearing in court without a coat than I was over the loss of my new coat. When I reached the courthouse, I immediately went to the public defender's office to seek out any willing lawyer to give me his coat to use for my court appearance. I met several fellow public defenders and asked somewhat sheepishly if I could borrow their coat. Unfortunately, each of them had court commitments, and all I received were their sympathies for my predicament. In somewhat desperate straits, I located one of our investigators who graciously offered me the use of his coat. I thanked him and quickly tried on the coat. Immediately, it was obvious to me that the coat was a very bad fit. It was tight around my shoulders, otherwise way too small, and the coat sleeves literally came up to my elbows.

The Court had always been strict and stringent about attorneys' attire in Court. In fact, I can remember several of them being reprimanded for not wearing a tie, one, unbelievably, for not having any socks, and one for not having a coat. I decided to choose the lesser of two evils and thought that a small coat is better than none at all. As I entered the courtroom, I tried not to be too sensitive about my appearance but purposely stood behind the tallest lawyers and their clients so as not to be too obvious. Fortunately, nothing was said to me but I could not help but wonder if any of the judges or lawyers thought that I had stopped at a surplus store on my way to court to buy such an ill-fitting suit coat.

During my first few years in the practice of law, no-fault divorce was not yet in effect. In order to obtain a divorce, a Master appointed by the Court would conduct a hearing to determine if there were grounds for the divorce. Usually, only the party seeking the divorce would appear, which would give that party much freer rein to expound on what had transpired during the marriage. In one of the first cases in which I was the Master, the husband testified that while he was out of town on a business trip, his separated wife found out the location where he was living and removed his entire clothing wardrobe including all of his shoes, slippers, and sneakers. She then without any qualms and in a charitable mood delivered them to a local Salvation Army center, where they were, in turn, distributed to those in need. Upon the husband's return, he was left with only the clothes on his back and was never able to recover any of the items taken although he did receive a credit for their value.

In another pre-no-fault divorce, I sat as the Master and heard a wife's testimony as to how her husband had made, in many ways, her life difficult and intolerable. She had been suffering from a pulmonary condition and had been instructed by her doctor to avoid smoke at all costs. When her lawyer asked her if she had informed her husband of her doctor's advice, she responded in the affirmative. When she was asked for his reaction, she responded in a mordacious manner that her bleeping husband had escalated his smoking by at least ten times when he was in her vicinity. No doubt, he was intent on pushing the envelope towards a final divorce.

In the final Master in divorce hearing that I conducted before the onset of no-fault divorce, the husband brought the divorce action against the wife on the grounds of adultery. The facts were relatively plain and simple, but the husband's reaction to what had transpired was both memorable and notable. The husband testified that his work shift had been changed from night shift to day shift. Upon completing his work for the day, he returned to his home and saw an unfamiliar truck in his driveway. He proceeded to enter the home, saw no one in either the kitchen or living room, and went towards the back bedroom. Upon opening the door, he saw his wife in bed with another man. His lawyer asked him, "Did you say anything to him? How did you react?" The husband in an animated and excited voice said, "Are you kidding, I didn't say a thing. He told me had a gun, and I ran out of the house as fast as I could."

In a subsequent divorce case, I represented a wife after the no-fault divorce act had been enacted and was in effect. After months of negotiations between the attorney for the husband and me, we finally reached agreement on all major terms except division of the items of personal property. As most lawyers would agree, sometimes the seemingly insignificant matters that involve household items or furnishings can prove to be the most problematical and can stretch out divorce proceedings when they should have been concluded a long time ago. One resolution to the dilemma in this case was to advise both clients to make out a list of what each wants and then simply attach it to the agreement as an exhibit. This happened to be a case where both parties took our advice literally. The list that they presented to both of us was the longest, most comprehensive personal property inventory I had ever seen in all my years practicing law. It was sixteen pages long, each page containing a his and a hers column. Some of the entries on the final page proved that they were intent on being fair and meticulous to a fault. A sample of my recollection of the submitted list follows:

HIS	**HERS**
Salt Shaker	Pepper Shaker
Toilet Brush	Toilet Brush Holder
Pens	Pencils
Square Potholders	Potholder Gloves
Toothpick Holders	Toothpicks
Patsy Cline Cassettes	Ray Charles Cassettes

The final items should indicate how long ago this case came to its "down to the penny" conclusion.

In 1975, I became a public defender on a per diem basis and, five years later, became a staff member of the Northampton County Public Defender's office. I was assigned to represent indigent persons who were facing criminal charges and continued in this capacity until 1998. During these twenty-three years, I encountered many serious cases where the defendants were facing the death penalty or life in prison. Fortunately, during these years, there were also humorous and lighthearted moments. Some of these instances occurred during the first phase of a criminal trial — jury selection. In my very first trial as a criminal defense lawyer, I was assigned to represent a fellow accused of stealing tires from a local gas station. In meeting with my client, I advised him that it would be in his best interest for him to wear appropriate clothing for the trial, not necessarily a coat and a tie, but clothes that were clean and presentable. Much to my consternation, he appeared on the day of the trial wearing a cutoff T-shirt, shorts, dirty sneakers, and no socks. His apparel obviously was in total contrast to what I had advised him. I asked the judge for a short delay, and an hour later, he appeared in decent clothes. During the trial, I addressed the jury for both opening and closing arguments, making sure each time that I spoke to them respectfully, starting with "Ladies and Gentlemen of the jury." The case was finally concluded, and unfortunately for the defendant and me, he was found guilty and I started my trial career with a loss. After the jury was dismissed, the Judge, rather sternly, asked me to approach the bench. He leaned over the bench and softly yet solemnly said, "Bill, for your first trial, you did a pretty good job but you made one glaring mistake." Mystified and nervously, I asked what error I had made. He then told me, while chuckling, that there were no women on the jury yet I had addressed them numerous times as Ladies and Gentlemen of the jury. I could only credit my embarrassing performance to a case of rookie butterflies and jitters. I resolved, from that moment on, to take proper account of the gender makeup of each jury in the future.

Several years later, I was representing a criminal defendant in an aggravated assault case. The jury pool of about sixty people entered the courtroom to be questioned by both the district attorney and myself as the criminal defense attorney. This questioning, known as voir dire, is used essentially to determine if any prejudice or bias exists among the prospective jurors. After the district attorney was through with his questioning, I stood up, faced the jury pool, and asked my typical first question: "Good morning, Ladies and Gentlemen, I am Attorney Bill Zaun and will be representing

Mr. Iam Guiltee who is seated to my right. I am a practicing attorney with a law office in Bethlehem. Do any of you know me?" One stocky gentleman far in the rear of the courtroom raised his hand. As soon as I looked at him, I knew that his face was familiar but I could not place him or figure out how I may have known him in the past. Acknowledging the juror, the Judge asked him, "How do you know Mr. Zaun?" His loud voice reverberated throughout the courtroom as he said, "I used to be on the chain gang with him." As ripples of laughter filled the courtroom, I remembered this fellow as being a co-worker for PennDOT when I worked with him one summer on the surveying crew. At the same time, I had a flashback of Paul Newman in the movie *Cool Hand Luke* dressed in black-and-white-striped prison gear and attached to the other prisoners by way of leg irons. Because of the excessive laughter in the courtroom, the Judge ordered a recess and called me into his chambers. I can still hear him telling me, "Bill, so that is what you do when business is bad, you work on the chain gang." The jury questioning continued and the trial resumed but I had a tough time afterwards, overcoming the juror's unintentional but funny remark.

On another occasion, I was assigned along with another defense lawyer to represent two men who were charged with particularly gruesome crimes in which the victim was severely beaten with a tire iron. I can easily recall the defendant that I was representing because of his slim stature and due to the fact that when the charges were initially filed and a warrant issued for his arrest, he tried to get away by riding a bicycle to New Jersey. His escape attempt was short lived as he was found a short time later. In any event, during our questioning of potential jurors we were trying to decide on which jurors to keep and which ones we should try to dismiss. One of the potential jurors identified himself as a football coach at a local high school. As he was being questioned by the district attorney, the other defense lawyer leaned over and whispered to me, "Bill, we better try and keep this guy on the jury; he's used to seeing people getting hit." So much for the inside scoop on picking jurors.

In another case, which involved a domestic dispute, I began picking a jury when the Judge asked members of the jury pool if they had any reason for not serving on the jury and, if it was a personal matter, that person should approach the bench and the Judge would address the person's concern. One woman raised her hand and said she had a personal conflict in serving on the jury. The Judge asked her and all of the lawyers to approach the bench. Once at the bench, the Judge inquired as to the nature of her conflict. She stated in distinct and alliterative terms, "I happen to be the best friend of Mr. Zaun's ex-wife." The Judge wistfully replied, "Enough said, you are dismissed from this case."

In 1987, I was assigned to a murder case, which because of all the pre-trial publicity was transferred to another county for the purpose of picking a jury. As the jury pool assembled, the Judge announced that he would be doing some preliminary questioning. After several questions, he asked the jurors if any of them had any problems with either their vision or their hearing. One woman, with very thick eyeglasses, responded that she had a problem with her sight. The Judge then asked, "Can you see me?" Her response was, "Yes, Your Honor, I can see you." The Judge then continued by asking the district attorney to stand and asked the lady, "Can you see the district attorney?" Her reply was, "Yes,

Your Honor, I can see the district attorney." Finally, the Judge asked me to stand up and asked the lady, "Can you see Mr. Zaun?" Her exact reply was, "Yes, Your Honor, I can see Mr. Zaun, but I can only see his head and his feet." The juror was dismissed by the Judge, but to this day, I do not understand her answer since I was standing in open view. I am sure the answer will forever remain a mystery.

One of the most common charges that my criminal defendant clients faced was driving under the influence charges. A most memorable moment occurred when I was assigned to represent an elderly man, Pete Pillpopper, who had driven his car off the side of the road and overturned and rolled into a ravine. After he received the summons in the mail, he came to see me to discuss the charges. As he walked into my office, I noticed that he was carrying with him a large paper bag that he set on my desk. He went on to explain that on the night he was arrested, he had not been drinking but was suffering from the side effects of all the medications he was taking. At this point, he opened the bag and dumped out its contents, revealing at least fifteen pill containers. He claimed that these were various prescribed medications being taken for several medical conditions from which he was suffering. Prior to driving that night, he told me that he had taken numerous pills that made him woozy while he was driving. I told him that I would obtain all the police reports pertaining to his accident and would review them prior to the preliminary hearing. In addition, I informed him that I would be checking into the nature of each of his medications and their possible side effects. I gave him the date of the preliminary hearing that I would meet him there and if there were any intervening developments that he should call me before the hearing. Sure enough, the night before the hearing, I received a call from Pete at home. His voice was animated and I could tell he was anxious to tell me something. He said that he had omitted some important facts when he came into my office and wanted to update me now. Curious as to what this important omission might be, I asked him what he had forgotten to tell me. He said that on the night that he took all the medications and prior to driving, he broke out in a rash that covered his whole body and caused itching that was unbearable. In order to relieve the itching, he said that he filled his bathtub with rubbing alcohol and soaked himself in it. He concluded that, as a result, the arresting officer smelled the rubbing alcohol and assumed that he was drinking. I knew that this was a rather bizarre explanation with no chance of success but told my client to get a good night's sleep and I would see him at the hearing.

The next day, at the hearing, the officer testified that upon finding my client's car, he noticed that the back seat and floor were littered with numerous empty liquor bottles and beer cans and further that my client was unsteady and reeked of alcohol. In my judgment, it was totally useless to even raise the rubbing alcohol defense, so I did not do so. The eventual outcome of the case was that my client pled guilty to a lesser charge of reckless driving, received a probationary sentence, and then told me he would never use rubbing alcohol again if he broke out in any rash. I must say that such a plea would not be allowed these days and rightfully so, but I believe that the district attorney had some sympathy for his age and for his disingenuous rubbing alcohol defense.

In what I regard as the singularly most embarrassing instance that I experienced as an attorney, I was assigned to represent a woman who faced serious charges of threatening a police chief with a loaded gun outside her home. In first interviewing the woman, it became clear to me that she had some serious mental health issues. While awaiting disposition of her case, she became disruptive in prison, damaged some prison property, and was aggressive and assaultive towards the prison guards. Her physical appearance lent credibility that she was a disturbed woman: obese, clearly unkempt, and inclined to speaking impulsively. Somehow, probably because of her mental health issues, I was able to negotiate a plea to a much lesser charge that would give her a chance to receive a probationary sentence, which would afford her minimal jail time. I informed the district attorney that we would be entering a guilty plea to the lesser charges and the date for her plea and sentencing was set for the first day of criminal court of the following month. On that date, I appeared with her in Courtroom #1, by far the most ornate and spacious courtroom in the courthouse. Being the first day of criminal court, the courtroom was packed to capacity, filled with district attorneys, defense attorneys, defendants waiting for their case to be called, and other interested onlookers. After the list had been called to determine the order in which the cases would be heard, the President Judge called my case for a guilty plea. I stood in the well of the courtroom, my client by my side and listened to the Judge spell out the charges to which my client was pleading guilty. He then proceeded to question my client in what lawyers know as the colloquy. "Mrs. Q., is your guilty plea free and voluntary?" Answer, "Yes, Your Honor." "Have any promises been made to you to enter your plea of guilty?" Answer, "No, Your Honor."

"Do you fully understand the charges to which you are pleading guilty?" Answer, "Yes, Your Honor." And then, the final question, "Are you satisfied with the services that your attorney has provided?" Answer, in an unmistakably loud and assured voice, "Your Honor, he has really serviced me well." The laugher in the courtroom was astounding. My face turned three shades of red and I wondered, *Does the courtroom have a trap door that I could suddenly fall into? Why did this happen to me?*

At the conclusion of the proceeding, I was surrounded by my chiding legal colleagues, some who provided conciliatory and consoling remarks and some who offered less than wanted remarks, such as, "Bill, now we know how you spend your free time" or "Bill, you devil." The comments truly overwhelmed me and I wondered to myself how long it would be until I revisited this courtroom. It was one of the very few times in my life that I was truly dumbfounded and speechless. My only hope after this traumatic experience was that the Court in the future would simply reword the colloquy and ask future defendants, "Has your lawyer done a good job?"

As I found out during my public defender years, sometimes our services go unappreciated or are not wanted at all. In a case I had before a local district justice, the defendant was known to wander about town aimlessly even during the winter months and would usually be arrested for loitering. When I began my representation of Ronnie Roamer, he had already spent a few months in prison and I did not believe that his outstanding charge warranted additional jail time. I discussed the matter with the district justice and he agreed, provided that in the future Mr. Roamer would not be an annoyance to his neighborhood. In Court, I asked that the charges be dismissed, provided that he abides by the Court's stipulation. The district justice dismissed the charges and announced, "Mr. Roamer, you are now a free man." Instantaneously, Mr. Roamer jumped out of his seat, turned to me, and said, "Mr. Zaun, you're fired." Surprised by his comment, I said, "Don't you want to get out of jail?" He said, "No, during the winter, I'd rather be in jail." I guess, in some instances, it is impossible to please a client.

One of the best scenarios that can truly help a criminal defense lawyer is overzealousness on the part of an arresting police officer. In just such a case, I represented a client, Tommy Toothorn, who was driving down a South Bethlehem street on a hot and steamy summer evening, when he saw several friends on the sidewalk, pulled over, and started beeping his horn acknowledging his friends' presence. The problem was that he continued the beeping until the police were called for a noise disturbance. On their arrival, one of the officers demanded that Tommy get out of his vehicle, put his hands on the roof of the car, while the officer patted him down. This officer, Stanley Strongarm, had a reputation for not being patient and for physically overreacting in certain situations. Once my client had his hands on the cruiser car roof he made some less than ingratiating comments to Officer Strongarm, and he then placed my client under arrest for disorderly conduct. When Tommy did not immediately comply with the officer's directives, he grabbed Tommy's arm, placed it against his back, and with an upward thrust, pushed it in such a fashion that he heard a crack. At that point, Tommy screamed in anguish and Officer Strongarm commented to his fellow police officer, "God……I broke his arm." Charges were subsequently filed, and after the preliminary hearing, the charges were bound over for Court. My client insisted on his innocence and asked that the case go to trial. At the trial, several months later, several witnesses gave testimony, and then Officer Strongarm was called to the stand. After asking him several questions about how this incident took place, I decided to go against the old defense adage of never asking a question that you do not know what the answer will be. Straightforwardly, I asked the officer, "Isn't it true that as you forced my client's arm behind his back and heard a cracking sound, you commented to your fellow officer, 'God……I broke his arm'?" His totally unexpected but most welcome response was, "That is absolutely untrue, what I said was, 'Son of a b…., I broke his arm.'" I took just one quick look at the jury as their smiles and laughs abounded, to know that this was a sure winner for the defense. I was right, the jury was out for only twenty minutes, hardly enough time to grab a cup of coffee, and came back with a verdict of not guilty, which thrilled my client and greatly displeased the district attorney. In this case, the officer's candid admission to injuring my client but his disagreement with the particular curse word provided the defense with a victory that I will long remember.

In a rather strange situation, I represented a defendant who was charged with burglary and theft. His evening began by imbibing at a local tavern frequented by a local college crowd. As he sat next to some of these students at the bar, he was able to glean information as to where these students lived. He left the bar, in a snowstorm, and walked to the apartment house where two of the college bar patrons lived. He was able to gain entry through a basement window and quickly found his way to the refrigerator on the first floor.

There, he located a full bottle of wine, ring bologna, and assorted cheeses. As he began to down the wine and have his own little party, one of the college roommates, who had not gone to the bar, heard some noises and thinking it was his roommate, hollered, "Is that you, Ralph?" Probably from indulging in too much wine, he incredulously gave his real name and said, "No, it's me, Eddie Eavesdropper." Immediately recognizing his mistake, he grabbed the wine, left the bologna and cheese, and ran down the steps and out the same basement window through which he had gained entry. He managed to walk through the snow and back to his own place about two blocks away. Once there, he fell into his bed and fell asleep with the wine bottle firmly clenched in his right hand. The police were called and were easily able to track down the culprit by following the footsteps in the snow. When they located Eddie, he was still engaged in his midwinter's night dream and once awakened was promptly arrested.

In another case having unusual circumstances, I was assigned to represent an individual who was charged with theft and receiving stolen property. In this particular case, an undercover state trooper set up a little store on the south side of Bethlehem. Word filtered around the community that you could go there and sell small items of stolen property. My client, Tony Trickster, entered the store with a stolen CD player and asked the state trooper, who was seated behind a desk, how much he would be willing to pay for the player. The trooper told him fifty dollars, and Tony gave him the player and received the fifty dollars. At that moment, the phone rang and the trooper answered the phone, which was located at the far end of the desk. While talking on the phone and looking out a window, Tony noticed a small radio (which just happened to be the trooper's own personal radio), grabbed it, and left the store while the trooper was still diverted, talking on the phone. Several hours later, in a display of unmatched brilliance and gall, Tony returned to the store and asked the trooper how much he would pay him for the radio. Quickly realizing it was his own radio, the trooper placed Tony under arrest. Several months later, without any real defense, Tony pled guilty to both charges and was sentenced to jail.

In an unusual case with both a comical and ironic ending, I was assigned to represent Harry Haveadouble, who was in prison on an assault charge involving an altercation at a neighborhood bar. Harry had already spent a month in prison awaiting disposition of his charges. At this time, I had a caseload of at least thirty cases, some of which had similar names such as Jones, Smith, etc. After lengthy negotiations with an assistant district attorney, we agreed to plead Harry guilty to a lesser charge of disorderly conduct, and the district attorney would recommend a time-served sentence, which meant Harry would not have to spend any more time in jail.

On the day of his guilty plea, I went to see the deputy sheriff in charge of the bullpen area where prisoners were kept temporarily until their case came before the judge. I asked the sheriff to please have Harry brought over to the courtroom so we could dispose of his case. When the person who I assumed was my client came over, I greeted him by saying, "Harry, I have some great news for you. I negotiated a plea to disorderly conduct and you should be able to be released from prison today." His facial expression was one of pure joy as he gave me a bear hug and thanked me over and over again. His moment of exhilaration was short lived when the deputy tapped me on the shoulder and informed me that they had brought over the wrong prisoner who just happened to have the same name but a different social security number and faced much more serious charges than my client, Harry Haveadouble. Needless to say, his ecstasy turned to agony as thc sheriff led him back to prison.

Back in the late 1970s, if a defendant wanted to represent himself, it was not uncommon for a judge to seek out a public defender who would act as standby counsel for the defendant. During criminal court week, I was walking to the law library when a Judge approached me and requested that I act as standby counsel for an individual charged with theft. The defendant would do all the talking and questioning during the trial, but I would be there to advise him on legal matters and to guide him through the trial procedures. In this case, as strange as it may sound, the defendant was charged with stealing a cow. Until that day, I did not know that cows were registered with the state. The specific cow was known as Holstein #18356. The District Attorney in this case was Nick Englesson, with whom I had had many cases in the past and with whom I enjoyed a good professional relationship.

The trial began and the defendant addressed the jury at opening arguments, questioned witnesses and, all in all, seemed to be doing a decent job. After testimony was closed and it was time for closing arguments, the Judge declared a recess in order that I could consult with the defendant and advise him on what closing comments he should make. We reentered the courtroom, and the Judge asked the defendant to begin his closing argument. He immediately began by walking towards the District Attorney and pointing at him while stating, "Ladies and Gentlemen of the jury, do you see this man: he looks like Al Pacino, he talks like Al Pacino, he even walks like Al Pacino; I think he thinks he is Al Pacino." Naturally, I was totally taken aback by his comments and wondered to myself — *Oh my god! I hope that Nick doesn't think that I told him to say that!* After the trial was over, I went over to Nick to assure him that I had nothing to do with the defendant's comments. He readily accepted my explanation, and to this day when we see each other, we share a laugh over this incident. I did, however, learn one axiom — when you are in Court, expect the unexpected.

As most attorneys know or have experienced, the practice of law is not without some danger not always in criminal cases but certainly in domestic cases. I personally encountered a degree of violence, and both were in domestic relations conferences. In the first such case, I was representing a wife who was challenging the amount of support that her husband was paying. The conference was held in a building separate from the courthouse, but each conference room had a somewhat elderly deputy sheriff posted outside the conference door. As the conference started, I was seated next to my client against the east wall, and her husband and his lawyer were seated across from us against the west wall. The female hearing examiner was seated behind her desk close to the north wall, and as we walked in the room, a civilian-dressed deputy sheriff was seated outside the door.

My client's contention was that she was receiving checks but not all the ones she was supposed to receive. As I reviewed copies of the checks, it was apparent to me that he was noting on the checks, for example, payment for January when, in actuality, it should have been for a prior month in which he did not make a payment. As I questioned him about the discrepancies, I could see him become increasingly annoyed, his voice suddenly got louder, and I saw his face turn apple red. I thought this was just an emotional reaction and began to look down at my notes, when suddenly he jumped up and raced towards me.

At this point, I saw him ready to swing at me, but all I could do was to throw my arms and hands in front of my face in an attempt to deflect his blows. He managed to hit me once but, fortunately, because I was able to react, I did not suffer any physical injury. What probably saved me from injury were his own lawyer's actions: jumping on him and keeping him at bay.

All the while that this was happening, the female hearing examiner was screaming at the top of her voice, "Sheriff! Sheriff!" To no avail. Unbeknownst to us, the deputy sheriff had departed for the men's room seconds before the husband's outburst and, therefore, was no help to any of us. The flustered hearing examiner declared the conference over and asked if I wanted to file any charges. I did file a police report so that there would be a record of his actions but left the matter end with that. I should add that this incident occurred prior to hearing officer's having panic alarms. The husband's lawyer apologized to me profusely and told me this would be the last time that he represents his client.

From this experience, I realized how volatile and potentially dangerous domestic matters could be. The second experience that I had with potential violence was also in a domestic relations conference. In this case, I was representing a father who was contesting the need to pay additional support for his boy's braces, which he claimed were not medically necessary but were for mere cosmetic purposes. At the conference, both counsel for the mother and I reviewed carious orthodontic reports — some claiming the need for braces and others stating that they were for cosmetic purposes only. As the hearing examiner was reviewing the reports, the mother, Victoria Vicious, got out of her seat and came over to me, screaming at me, "You don't think he needs these braces?" and again, "You don't think he needs these braces? Well, here you are!" With that, she pulled out her son's impressions from her purse and snapped them directly in front of my nose barely missing an extraction of part of my nose. Had I been Pinocchio, my entire nose would have been gone. My advice for any lawyers involved in a case involving the need for braces is "Brace yourself for those braces."

One of the most serious cases I became involved with concerned the murder of an elderly woman by a former housekeeper. The housekeeper had worked for the victim for several months, but soon she became disenchanted with her work habits and fired her. Already beset by serious mental health issues, the housekeeper gradually became more and more depressed and was unable to eat or sleep properly. Living by herself in a tawdry and run-down motel, she decided to walk to her former employer's home even though it was some distance away, in a pouring rainstorm, to ask for a recommendation for future employment. When she finally arrived, umbrella in hand, she asked and implored the elderly woman to give her a favorable recommendation so that she could obtain employment. When the homeowner was adamant that she was not about to give her the recommendation, the former housekeeper became angered and struck the woman in her rib cage with her umbrella.

As a result of the assault, the victim died from the complications that ensued from a collapsed lung. After being charged with criminal homicide, she filed an application for a public defender, and shortly thereafter, another criminal defense lawyer and I were assigned to represent her. After several discussions, we jointly decided that we needed to gather as much information as possible about her background. Luckily, our investigator found out that she had been married and was now divorced. We were able to track down the former husband who was still living in the former marital home and ordered a deposition to take place at the courthouse. After some preliminary questions, I asked the former husband if his former wife ever acted strangely. Without pausing, he told us that it was not at all uncommon for his former wife, while he was at work, to grab a chain saw from the garage and cut down numerous trees in their backyard. I then asked him, "Well, I assume you lived on a wooded lot?" He was quick to reply, "Not anymore I don't." The eventual outcome of the case was that the defendant pled guilty but mentally ill and received a sentence, part of which was served in a mental institution. The case was a sad one for all involved, but I will long remember the former husband's telling remark.

As a criminal defense lawyer, it is often difficult to recall many of the cases in which you were involved, but unusual court sentences of criminal defendants are something long remembered. Such was the case in which the defendant, Mary Wide, was charged with prostitution. As I recall the facts, she was working the streets of downtown Easton, when she flagged down an Easton district justice, solicited him for sex, and was immediately driven by the district justice to the local police station. She subsequently entered a guilty plea and, at the time of sentencing, told the Judge that she was from San Antonio, Texas. I vividly remember the Judge in pronouncing her sentence as follows: "You are hereby ordered to leave town by sundown. The probation office is ordered to provide you with a one-way bus ticket to San Antonio, Texas." I thought for a moment that I was back in the Wild West at the turn of the 19th century. In any case, the defendant appeared to be pleased with the sentence and happily complied. Incidentally, the guilty plea took place in December near Christmastime, and I clearly remember other public defenders wishing me "A Mary Wide Christmas."

In one case with unique circumstances or, as you will see, unique consequences, I was assigned to represent a young woman, Ingrid Indiscreet, who was arrested and charged with the crime of open lewdness. The facts of the case were as follows: my client and a young man, during the early hours of the morning, were engaged in sexual intercourse in front of their second-floor apartment. Both of them were totally nude. An elderly woman who resided on the floor below them, happened to open her door to retrieve her morning newspaper, when in shocking disbelief, she witnessed the gyrations and antics of the couple on the second-floor landing. She immediately closed the door and called the police. Minutes later, on hearing the blaring police sirens, they ran into their apartment and out a window that led to a small landing which had a low railing.

As the police were pulling up to the residence, my client stood there ostensibly, afraid to jump while her sexual cohort, Freddy Fearless, decided to leap to freedom. He landed in a large sticker bush, the needles of which adhered to his body, making him look like an oversized porcupine. As he screamed in anguish, the police grabbed a large blanket from the police cruiser trunk and covered Freddy with it. He was arrested for open lewdness and criminal mischief (damage to the sticker bush) while my client was charged with open lewdness only. Hearings were held separately for both of them. At the hearing for my client, Ingrid, the first-floor female witness failed to appear. The arresting officer, however, did appear and testified to seeing both Ingrid and Freddy on the landing in the nude. Since in a charge for open lewdness, the Commonwealth must show that the defendant's appearance or conduct caused an affront or alarm to the witnessing person, I asked the officer (known for his liberal leanings) if he had ever seen any pornographic movies and, if so, was he alarmed or affronted by viewing them? His forthright answer was that, yes, he had seen a pornographic movie in the past and, no, he was not alarmed or affronted by his viewing of them. I, then, went on to ask if he was affronted or alarmed by seeing my client in her state of undress and his answer was no. Since the Commonwealth had no other witnesses to present, I asked that the charges be dismissed. My motion was granted, and Ingrid walked away, free and unscarred.

During my years as a criminal defense attorney, one of the most frequently committed crimes was that of retail theft. If the offense was a first instance by the defendant or was less than $150.00, the case would be treated as a summary offense and would be heard by a magisterial district judge. However, if the offense was a subsequent offense over the statutory limit, the crime would be considered a misdemeanor or felony and would proceed through the County Court system.

I found that the motivation for this type of crime is either to obtain items for which the defendant does not have the financial means to pay for them or to sell the items for cash to purchase illicit drugs.

In one particular retail theft case, with an almost hard to believe comical ending, I represented an individual, Sammy Steppinglitely, who entered a supermarket after having had a couple too many beers. He entered the store at night within an hour of closing time and proceeded to the rear of the store where a storage area was located. In this room, he found a ladder that was used to gain access to a loft area. His plan of action was to sleep for a while and then to go to the lower level and pick out some of the most expensive items and leave the store before it would open the next morning. Unfortunately, for Sammy, he did not have the foresight to bring with him an alarm clock. He snoozed comfortably and unabated through the night, and when he awoke, he could hear the sounds of customers on the supermarket floor wheeling their shopping carts and buying their groceries. Alarmed by his failed plan, he began to walk along the ceiling of the store not knowing that it was a false ceiling. Sammy only made it a couple of steps when he fell through the ceiling and unbelievably fell into the shopping cart of a shocked and unsuspecting female shopper. The force of his landing overturned the shopping cart and caused Sammy to suffer a broken leg in the process. Fortunately, the female shopper was not injured, but one can only imagine her horror and probable belief that the sky was falling. My recollection is that it took quite some time for the preliminary hearing to be held because of Sammy's hospitalization. I do recall, however, that when the preliminary hearing was finally held, the Judge imposed a bail release condition barring Sammy from the store including both the main floor and the area from which Sammy fell.

In another retail theft case, this one without any injuries, I represented a man in his twenties, Willie Wrangler. This case took place prior to the sophisticated surveillance cameras that are now commonplace in virtually every large store. Willie entered the department store and proceeded to the men's clothing area where he perused various types of jeans on display. He selected four pairs of jeans, ironically or suitably, each one size larger than the other. He proceeded to the changing area and in sequence put on the smallest size first, then the next larger size until, in an amazing feat of leg dexterity, he had wearing on his person four pairs of jeans. Upon leaving the dressing room area, an observant clerk noticed Willie's stifled and troubled gait and summoned security who were able to unravel the mystery of Willie's slow and tedious walk once he left the dressing area. This case points out the lengths and widths that some people are willing to go to in order to secure their fashion desires.

Midway through my years as a public defender, some of the staff were given additional responsibilities besides representing defendants in criminal cases. I was asked to undertake representation of people who were about to be or were committed to a mental facility, in some cases, where they had threatened suicide or were suffering from some psychosis, schizophrenia, etc. I must say that I have to this day, a lot of empathy for mental-health patients since, in some cases, their disease is of a long-standing nature and also very debilitating. On the day that I was to encounter my first mental-health hearing, I had some trepidation, not knowing what to expect or what they would be like. As I entered the mental-health facility, I approached the nurse in charge and inquired as to where my client was located so that I could speak to her before the hearing. The nurse directed me to her room, but on the way there, she warned me to be careful and said that the female patient was a "shark." Not wanting to appear unprepared, I did not ask the nurse any further questions.

Being a neophyte in this area, I thought that maybe the nurses had some internal rankings for patients or designations such as tadpole, fish, etc. When I finally entered the patient's room, I went over to her bedside and introduced myself to her, telling her the reason that I was there. Immediately and without warning, she snapped out at me and attempted to bite me, just barely missing my hand, which I had placed on her bed rail. Suddenly, I realized the import of the nurse's warning and felt somewhat ignorant that I had not understood what she had meant.

On another occasion, I was going to attend a mental-health hearing, and as I arrived in the parking lot, it began raining heavily. I had come prepared, wearing a raincoat but, inadvertently, forgot my umbrella. By the time I entered the facility, my hair was soaking wet and my raincoat drenched. I went up to the third floor, and as I was walking towards the nurses' station, I noticed a gentleman dressed in hospital-patient attire rapidly approaching me. By the time he finally stopped, we were practically face-to-face. He asked me if it was raining outside which I thought to be a bit odd since I was soaking wet. Nevertheless, I answered him and said,

"Yes, it is." He then asked me rather demandingly and quite forcefully, "What's the wind velocity?" I thought to myself, *No one has ever asked me that question.* Not wanting to upset the man, I thought I would be a little creative and said, "It's eight miles out of the northwest." He quickly responded by saying, "You're full of s---; it is ten miles out of the southeast." I went on my way, thinking, *From now on I'll have to be more attentive to the weather report when I leave for work.*

The last mental-health hearing that left me with some memorable moments occurred when I was assigned to represent a woman who had already been in a mental-health facility for thirty days. She was now scheduled to have a hearing to determine whether or not she should be committed for an additional period of ninety days. When I first saw the woman in the interview room prior to the hearing, she was well dressed, neatly groomed, and seemed to be very pleasant. As I began to talk to her, I sensed that she might not belong there and was determined to do all that I could to obtain her release. She insisted that I had to get her out because she needed to get back to her business. I asked her what type of business she owned and where it was located. She answered emphatically and said that she owned a conglomerate in Czechoslovakia that had a satellite office on the Hudson River in New York. Immediately, the red flag went up but I assured her that I would represent her well. We entered the hearing room and the Master introduced himself and explained the procedures to be followed at the hearing. Unexpectedly, she spoke up and in a resolute and resounding voice said, "I don't want Mr. Zaun to represent me. I want to represent myself." The Master advised against this course of action, cautioning her that it might be difficult for her to conduct a cross-examination of the doctor and the other attending witnesses. However, she persisted and the hearing went on with her asking the questions and making statements while I sat behind her in silence. At the conclusion of the hearing, the Master said, "Ma'am, it is abundantly clear that you need further mental-health treatment, and I, therefore, commit you for an additional period of ninety days." She then jumped out of her seat, did an about-face, and quite vehemently said to me, "You rotten s.o.b., you lost my case." Dumbfounded by the logic of the response, but not wanting to insult her in any way, I wished her well and thought to myself, *This is the first time I've lost a case in which I didn't even represent a client.*

In 1998, I ended my role as a public defender and returned to private practice, this time in Egypt, North Whitehall Township, Pennsylvania.

In the late summer in 2001, while making purchases at a local store in Northampton, I was told by a police officer that District Justice Harold Weaver, who had served as District Justice in Lehigh Township for as long as anybody could remember, and who may have had the longest tenure as a magistrate and then district judge in Northampton County, was retiring in July. Therefore, there would be a vacancy in the office until the next municipal election, which would have to be filled by a gubernatorial appointment. His comments piqued my interest, and I began to give serious thought to seeking this appointment. After several days and nights of discussions with my wife, Til, I decided to seek the Governor's appointment. After numerous interviews with local politicians, and discussions with the Governor's office,

I was notified that the State Senate had unanimously approved Governor Tom Ridge's recommendation that I be appointed as District Justice for District Court 03-3-91. On November 9, 2001, I was sworn into office by then President Judge Robert Freedberg. I must admit that with my family members present and so many friends who had helped along the way, I felt a sense of gratitude, exhilaration, and a determination to serve my district as best I could.

Chapter Eight

Years of Judicial Decision Making

Prior to taking office, I was notified by the Court Administrator's office that I would need to be fitted for my new judicial robe. I went for the fitting and was told that I would be called in three weeks when it was ready. I received the phone call as predicted three weeks later and was told, "Mr. Zaun, your gown is ready for you to pick up." At that moment, reality struck home and I realized that I was about to embark on a totally different aspect of my professional life. As I previously mentioned, my appointment was to fill a vacancy created by the retirement of my predecessor, District

Justice Harold Weaver. In the interim period between his retirement and my appointment, all the summonses and notices of hearings were mailed out with the office being designated on the forms as "District Justice Vacant." On the first day that I took office, I was scheduled for a full slate of hearings beginning at 9 a.m. After donning the robe for the first time and conducting my first hearing, I was on my way to my secretary's desk to deliver my disposition of the hearing when a woman, who had just come in the front door, walked up to me and said, "Excuse me, are you District Justice Vacant?" What an auspicious start!

I soon became accustomed to my new role as a decision maker rather than an advocate. One person who would have preferred that I stay in my former position as a lawyer was a man arrested for stealing a milk truck and taking the cash proceeds from the truck. The police arrested him and brought him to my office so that I could arraign him, inform him of the charges, and set his bail. While asking him questions that would help me determine the amount of bail, I began to think that I might have represented him a long time ago as a public defender. I finally set his bail at $10,000.00, and he was not at all pleased, at first grumbling that he should not have been arrested at all and then mumbling about the inequities in the judicial system. After completing and signing all of the appropriate paperwork, the police began to escort him out of the office, when one of the officers said that the defendant would like to say something before he leaves. I said, "Sure, go right ahead." His indignant reply, "Judge, you know what, you should have stayed a f...... lawyer." The police then asked whether I would like to increase his bail because of his attitude and untimely remarks. I said, "No, just enjoy your trip to the prison."

The jurisdiction of my district included Lehigh Township, Moore Township, and the boroughs of Walnutport and Chapman. It is situated in the northwest corner of Northampton County and is close to the adjoining borders of both Carbon and Lehigh counties. The composition of the populace in this district is truly diverse with many agricultural interests, farmers, auto dealers, commercial complexes, trailer parks, and other business enterprises.

In one of the more uncommon cases that I heard in the first year of my term, a person was driving up a highway in the township when his truck was struck by a guinea hen, which had left a farmer's nearby property. The resulting accident caused damage to the driver's truck, and he subsequently filed suit against the farmer. On the day of his hearing, the truck owner and his attorney entered the courtroom first, followed by the farmer's attorney, and then the farmer. His attorney had instructed him prior to the day of his hearing to bring with him anything that would be helpful to his defense. When the farmer entered the courtroom, he was carrying a large paper bag. His attorney asked him what he had in the bag and the farmer replied, the dead guinea hen. His attorney truculently said, "Get that thing the hell out of here." I assume that the guinea hen was not the sort of evidence the farmer's attorney had in mind or expected.

Hoping not to give the impression that the cases that I heard as a district justice were mainly involving poultry and animals (although I did hear numerous dog cases), one had a unique twist. In this case, a homeowner's dogs had left the premises of the owner and had made their way to a farmer's henhouse, where at least twenty chickens were housed, fed, and maintained. The dogs were somehow able to gain entry to the henhouse and the onslaught began. The homeowner was charged under the Pennsylvania Dog Law with not having the dogs properly confined. The owner of the deceased and injured chickens at the hearing for the purpose of not only testifying to the facts, but also to pursue his claim for restitution for his losses, presented documents indicating where and when he had purchased the poultry and the cost of each dead or maimed chicken. He, then, went on to insist on restitution based not only on the loss of the chickens but also an amount representing the loss of productivity of each chicken. His calculations, which filled numerous pages, were based on his estimation of how many eggs the chickens would have laid during their lifespan. This claim was novel to me and raised in my mind the following questions: Do chickens lay the same amount of eggs each day? Do they have bad days when they don't lay any eggs? Can other factors such as barking dogs or stormy weather interfere with their ability to lay eggs or, at least, decrease their egg-laying output? What is the life expectancy of these chickens? Having not been provided with answers to these questions, I granted the farmer's claim for the destroyed and injured chickens and denied his in future claim for the lost egg productivity.

One of the other functions of a magisterial district judge is to assess fines, issue warrants, and hold payment determination hearings to determine if an individual has the ability to pay the fines and costs and warrant fees. If the determination is that the defendant can pay, an arrangement can be made whereby he or she would make weekly, bi-weekly, or monthly payments until the fines and costs have been paid in full. In one instance, an individual was brought into my office by the constable pursuant to a warrant that had been issued for this person since he had not abided by the terms of the payment agreement. Shortly after his arrival, his mother came in to offer support to her son. After reviewing his record of non-compliance, I told him that jail might be the only option because of the inordinate total amount of unpaid fines and costs. His slender, frail, elderly mother, clearly in her eighties, stepped forward, and as soon as she heard the word "jail" for her son, she pleaded with me not to send him to prison. Ordinarily, under the above circumstances, I would send the defendant to jail and the time spent there would then abrogate the fines and costs. However, in this instance, because of the high amount of the outstanding fines and costs, the defendant was looking at substantial time in prison. When the mother noticed that her plea for leniency was not affecting my thought process in making a decision, her voice began trembling, her hands shaking, and her eyes filled with tears. She then said as forcefully as she could, "Judge, if you send my son to prison, my blood will forever be on your hands." Suddenly, I recalled my grandfather many years ago, issuing me a reprimand in the following words, "If you don't knock it off, your hand is going to stick out of the grave." But, I had never heard him or anyone else, for that matter, alluding to me having blood on my hands. I must admit that her emotion-filled plea and her prophecy of impending doom struck some latent, responsive chord within me, so I decided to allow the defendant to pay half of the total due and the remaining balance in three months.

At some hearings, either the prosecution or defense will request that a video be played for the purpose of giving more clarity to a certain point or to show the alleged scene of the crime. In a case before me, the prosecution asked to show a high-speed chase that, in turn, became a low-speed chase. The chase was precipitated by a person traveling at a high rate of speed and, then, failing to stop when police overhead lights and sirens were activated. After several unsuccessful attempts to catch up to the alleged violator, the police finally followed him into a cul-de-sac. The police employed the use of a loudspeaker and several times shouted in the direction of the defendant, "Push the brake," "Push the brake." The defendant failed to comply and like a merry-go-round kept going around the cul-de-sac. Because of his now slow rate of speed, the police were able to get a good look at his face as was depicted on the video. Finally, the police officer, with an abundance of patience, again shouted, "Push on the brake," "Stop." The driver then, brazenly and quite disingenuously, rolled down his window and yelled, "I don't understand English." He then quickly drove out of the cul-de-sac, sped down the highway, and later ditched the car and ran. No arrest was made that night, but, a few days later, the police apprehended the suspect and were able to make a positive identification. After the hearing, the case was bound over for Court. Once again proving the old adage "a picture (or, in this case, a video) is worth a thousand words."

My appointment to the position of Magisterial District Justice was from November 2001 to January 4, 2004. In early 2003, I made the decision that I would run for election for a six-year term. I had never run for an elective office before (unless you would include my sophomore year in the high-school election disaster) and was not sure what a campaign would entail, although I was determined to put forth my best effort to ensure my election. My opponent was a long-serving and well-known police officer in Lehigh Township with deep roots in the community. I knew that name recognition would be a very important factor. Both my wife and I were Bethlehem natives and did not move to Lehigh Township until 1991. Up until 2001, I had maintained a law practice in Bethlehem and then North Whitehall Township.

I initially sent a letter to almost all of the constituents in my district and then followed it up with several mailings containing my brochure, which described my background and reasons for seeking office. I had a lot of assistance from family and friends who put in countless hours preparing for the election. I still knew that the above would not be enough, so I set out on a course whereby I would try to go door to door as many nights and weekends as I could in order to personally introduce myself to the electorate. My door-to-door plan was not as easy as it first seemed. In my district, there are many farms, and because of its rural complexion, many homes are far apart from each other. Energy and perseverance were another concern.

I can remember one evening, when I had had a full day of hearings and then went door to door to just about sunset. I called my wife and told her that was enough for tonight, then she sweetly asked and enticed me to go to ten more homes for her and then call it quits for the night. I think I went to eleven more homes that night (probably for extra credit), but it was this type of encouragement and her positive support that kept me going.

One item that I had not considered before going door to door was the presence of large dogs. While on the campaign trail, I encountered more large dogs in homes or in their yards than I had in my lifetime. I clearly remember one such dog actually breaking through a window and chasing me as I ran back to the car. That experience conjured up memories of the time I had worked for my father and was delivering two wrapped turkeys to a home on the outskirts of Bethlehem. By mistake, I went to the wrong home of a well-known builder who had written a letter to the editor of the local newspaper stating something to the effect that if any intruders or unwanted business solicitors were to come to his house unannounced, they would be met by two ferocious German shepherds. Talk about bad directions and timing! I drove up the driveway leading to the house and stopped the delivery truck. As soon as I left the truck with the two wrapped turkeys, I saw two large German shepherds heading towards me, probably hell-bent on devouring me. At that point, I decided that discretion is the better part of valor, threw the turkeys to the dogs, and got out of there as fast as I could. After the campaign incident with the dog chasing me, I instituted my own policy of self-preservation campaigning, whereby if I saw a large barking dog at a home, I would simply pass that home and say to myself, "Chalk that one up for my opponent," and move on to the next home.

During my door-to-door adventures, I remember approaching a farmhouse that seemed like it was out in the wilderness. When I got to the door, I saw a large sign above the door that stated, "NO SOLICITORS ALLOWED." When the owner pulled back the curtain on the door, I could see he was not thrilled with me being there. I tried to introduce myself and even held up and waved some of my campaign literature containing my picture, but to no avail. In a raspy and bellowing tone, he shouted, "What the hell is the matter with you, buddy — can't you read the sign?" I figured no way was I going to get his vote, got back in my car, and tried to drive back to civilization.

On another door-to-door visit to a potential voter's home, I rang the doorbell and soon a woman appeared at the door and before I could say a single word, she said, "I can't tell you how happy I am to see you. I've been waiting over an hour for you to get here and you're finally here!" I thought, *What a receptive voter. I'm guaranteed her vote but then*, I wondered, *how on earth did she know that I was coming?* I told her that I was running for District Justice, would answer any questions, and would appreciate her vote. Her facial expression led me to believe that I had burst her bubble and I was right. She said, "Oh my God, I've been without phone service for the last two hours, and I thought you were here from Verizon to fix my phone." After displaying such disappointment, I figured the only way I would ever get her vote was if I repaired her phone, which I had neither the wherewithal nor the inclination to do.

On Saturday morning, still being in the door-to-door campaign mode, I ventured out, even though it was raining steadily. This time, I did come prepared with an umbrella (even though I rarely use them because I usually lose them) and started up the walkway to the voter's home. Halfway up the walk, with my umbrella up, I walked through a wooden trellis that was stationed over the walk. As I did, the umbrella got caught and struck in the wooden slats of the trellis. As I pulled and tugged on the umbrella trying to dislodge it, I could see the resident at the large picture window looking at me with a quizzical expression that soon turned to laughter. Minutes later with a damaged umbrella and now soaking wet, I finally reached the doorstep and was greeted by the female onlooker. I explained that I was campaigning for District Justice. I am sure she could not resist making the comment, "I sure hope your job does not require you to use an umbrella."

Probably the most unforgettable campaign stop I made occurred when I was asked by a couple to officiate at their renewal of wedding vows at a local rod and gun club. I had never been to this establishment before and was uncertain where I had to go to perform the ceremony. I used the one entrance, carrying my robe on a hanger, and found there were already many attendees already there. I asked the manager where I could change into my robe and he directed me to an adjacent room. When I entered, I saw a room filled with pool tables, shuffleboards, and a long bar filled with patrons. As I put on my robe, a young barmaid came from behind the bar and walked up to me and said, "Excuse me, are you a priest?" I said, "No." She then asked, "Are you a minister?" I said, "No." To end the suspense, I told her that I was the local District Justice and that I was seeking election for another term. She said, "Well, guess what, your opponent is my cousin." I replied by saying that I was glad to meet her. She then leaned closer and said, "Do you mind if I tell you something?" Intrigued, I said that I did not. She then said with a wry grin, "You know, you are much better looking in your campaign brochure than you are in person." Realizing that I had just received a totally unbiased opinion, I said, "Thank you very much," and posthaste proceeded to the room to perform the renewal of the vows ceremony.

My campaign finally came to a successful end on Election Day in November of 2003, as I was elected to a six-year term concluding on January 4, 2010. One of the many duties of a District Justice is the performance of wedding ceremonies. Initially, I would perform these ceremonies for anyone requesting them, provided that they had the proper county marriage license. Later on, I limited these ceremonies to those people in my district who would come to my office, usually on Friday afternoons. I made this change because I did not want to become a traveling wedding minister, having received all types of requests, e.g. marriage on a small island in the middle of a lake.

During the course of officiating at hundreds of weddings, a few are highlighted in my memory. At one particular ceremony, the courtroom was packed with the bride and groom's relatives and friends. It was the second marriage for both parties, and the bride and groom approached the middle of the courtroom for me to perform the ceremony. At the part of the ceremony where I say, "If anyone has any objection to the union of these two people, state the objection now or forever hold your peace," a little boy, probably age five or six, came running up to his mother who was the bride-to-be and shouted, "Mom, don't do it. Mom, please don't do it." This happening was a novel one for me, having only seen it in some old movie. I tried to disregard the comment so as not to embarrass the bride and groom and disrupt the ceremony. I thought, in retrospect, that had it been an adult objecting, I would have had to hear the objection and rule on it before proceeding with the ceremony. Fortunately, I never faced this scenario again.

At another wedding ceremony, I had the bride and groom come forward for the ceremony. I would always use the printed-out, formatted ceremony that my predecessor had used and did so in this instance. However, in reading the words used in the ceremony, I inadvertently and embarrassingly skipped a line so that the words read as follows: THIS

IS NOT A UNION THAT SHOULD BE ENTERED INTO UNADVISEDLY OR SOBERLY. Immediately, all who were present began laughing and I can recall the groom quipping that I probably read the right words. After this occurrence, I had my secretary retype the ceremonial words in the largest letter size available so that this would not happen again.

At yet another ceremony, the prospective bride was an immigrant who seemed to understand English but had trouble speaking it and did so with a somewhat heavy accent. When I got to the part of the ceremony where the rings were exchanged, I said to the bride, "As you place this ring on the groom's hand, repeat after me: Receive this ring as a treasure that I now give you." Her repetition was as follows: "Receive this ring with the pleasure that I will now give you." The ensuing look on the groom's face was truly priceless. Never before, and never again, will a bride and groom leave a courtroom after being married with such speed and such a sense of urgency!

During the course of my service as a District Justice, I have encountered, as might be expected, all types of individuals, from all walks of life. These would include, but are not limited to, police officers, dog wardens, game commissioners, pilots, doctors and nurses, car dealers, landlords, tenants, schoolteachers, students, farmers, store owners, secretaries, technicians, attorneys, paralegals, housewives, and even some self-professed global warming experts. For the most part, the great majority have shown respect for the Court both inside and outside the courtroom. They would address me as Judge, Your Honor, Magistrate, and some hailing back to the good old days, Squire. Of course, I have been addressed by others who referred to me as "the tall guy," "the man in the back," "dude," and some very few who have used expletives that I will not repeat here. One especially irreverent soul referred to me as "Bozo." However, these instances have been few and far between and usually come from individuals unhappy with a decision or with life in general.

Without being too introspective, one of my most obvious faults as a District Justice has been to confuse relationships. When people come into the District Court Office to take care of a warrant, to institute a payment plan, or to plead guilty or not guilty to a traffic offense, it has been my normal practice to have them sit on chairs at the counter portion of the office and will then call them up as their respective paperwork is ready. I have already asked a gentleman to come forward and said, "Your mother can come up here, too," only to find out by him telling me, "That's my wife." On another occasion, I have said to a woman, again without knowing, "Your sister can come up here with you," only to find out that it is her girlfriend. By the end of my term, I decided that I would no longer assume the nature of any relationship unless I was absolutely sure of it.

A District Justice has numerous duties such as conducting criminal preliminary hearings to determine whether the case should be dismissed or bound over to county court, civil cases involving disputes under $8,000, landlord-tenant disputes, executions on personal property, arraignments, setting bail, administering oaths of office to elected officials, and performing wedding ceremonies. One which has gone unmentioned and was personally the least liked was night duty. When a person is arrested for a misdemeanor 1 or 2 level or a felony, after court hours of 4:30 p.m. to 9:00 a.m., the following day or on weekends, he must appear before the District Justice for arraignment and for setting bail. The District Justice also must handle, after hours, emergency protection from abuse matters, indirect criminal contempt for violation of a protection-from-abuse order, and arraignment of those arrested for being a fugitive from justice. My predecessor, Harold Weaver, now deceased, called it his least liked duty and, when retiring, something he was glad to do without. I echo those sentiments wholeheartedly.

When I first began as District Justice, the system in our county consisted of the night-duty district justice being equipped with a pager (which I would rather refer to as that bleeping incessant noisemaker). When the District Justice would be paged, he would have to leave his home, drive to the office, prepare all the paperwork, and then arraign the defendant. I could recall many times on a cold, wintry night, finishing an arraignment and starting to drive home. It was as if the pager knew where I was because, invariably, the pager would beep when I was within one hundred yards of my home, necessitating a trip right back to the office.

I can remember, several years ago, being paged when we were experiencing a blinding snowstorm and being unable to get out of my driveway. Luckily, the police were able to pick me up in the police van with several police officers and the defendant himself and drove us to the office for the arraignment. On another nasty night, I was called out for an emergency protection-from-abuse matter. Just as I arrived at the office and was unlocking the door, I heard an unforgettable thud that appeared to be coming from Route 248, yards from my office. I alerted the police officer who had just arrived, and he went to Route 248 to investigate. After he did not return, I decided to walk to the point where I thought the thud had occurred. Lo and behold, an elderly male driver of a Hyundai had just struck a HORSE who had bolted from the horse farm, which is next to the District Justice office. The horse died immediately, and the elderly male driver lay there, inundated with glass, bleeding profusely. The police and EMS workers were attending to him and had to call for his transport by medivac to the hospital. I remember praying for him that night, and I did later learn that he had survived but had taken over one hundred stitches to his face and neck. There was absolutely no humor in this situation, but after this accident whenever I was called out on night duty, I drove slowly and alertly, always leery that another horse might bolt out while I was driving.

Several years later through the efforts of the President Judge and others in Court Administration, the system was changed by installing video-conferencing equipment in each District Judge's home, which was linked to two booking centers, where defendants would be arraigned. This change made night duty much more palatable and was a true blessing for each District Justice.

The change in the night-duty system from office to home did not change the frequency of the pager's beeping. If I would decide to go to bed at 10 p.m., the beeper would go off at 10:10 p.m. If I would wait up until midnight, without fail, the pager would go off at 12:15 a.m. I finally decided that there was only one real resolution to this devilish dilemma and that was to make two large pots of coffee, stay up all night, and become Rip Van Winkle once night duty was over. I do recall some instances on night duty, however tiresome, that left me with some enjoyable remembrances.

One night, the police had arrested a woman for driving under the influence and reckless driving. She was taken to the booking center, and I was alerted by way of the pager that she was ready to be arraigned. When I got on screen with her, I pulled out my standard set of questions that I used for every defendant, including age, residence, relatives that live in the area, financial considerations, i.e., do they own property or have bank accounts, any addictions, any failures to appear in court and, finally, any prior convictions. I could tell it was going to be a long night, when after asking her name and address, I asked her how old she was. Her answer, "Judge, I am as old as the speed limit." Engagingly, I asked her, "Well, were you driving on Route 248, the PA Turnpike, or 1-78?" Her well-thought-out answer was, "It was none of those, so I guess I'm forty." The next set of questions and her answers to them were just as unresponsive, so I committed her to prison and went back for another cup of coffee.

Yet another interesting arraignment on night duty occurred when I was paged to do an arraignment for a man who had been arrested for driving under the influence, careless driving, and stop-sign violations. When he got on screen, I asked him his name, address, and age. He answered fine until I got to the question pertaining to addictions. I asked him if he had any addictions to alcohol, drugs, gambling, or had any mental issues. He replied, "None." I then asked him if he had ever been convicted of a crime. His answer was no. I called on the officer to review his rap sheet to see if his answer was truthful. The officer said that he had six prior convictions for driving under the influence. I asked the defendant if he had simply, and conveniently, forgotten these convictions. He said, "I had two in Tennessee, two more in Kentucky, and two in Florida, and I didn't think those counted because I'm in Pennsylvania now, right?" I said in response, "You are right that you are now in Pennsylvania but, unfortunately, that is all you are right about." I, then, committed him to prison and went back for what I hoped would be my final cup of coffee for the night.

Chapter Nine

The Beginning of Retirement

In January 2009, it was decision-making time for me. My elective term would expire on January 4, 2010. The dilemma I faced was that if I decided to run for reelection and succeeded, I would be reelected to a six-year term ending in January 2016. Because of the minor judiciary mandatory retirement age of seventy, I could only serve two years of the six-year term. In that event, in February 2012, the office would become vacant, necessitating an appointment by the Governor until the next municipal election. In my honest assessment, I felt that this would be an injustice to the constituents of my district. I then decided not to run for reelection and to retire at the end of my term on January 4, 2010.

I must say that the humor has not departed since my retirement. No one has as of this date referred to me as "OLD MAN" or "POP." However, the other day, about two days after my retirement, I went to a local store for coffee and a newspaper. The male clerk behind the counter, I am sure without any ill intention, and in a nice way, said, "Judge, are you unseated yet?"

The last time I remember hearing or seeing that term is when, in some foreign country, the head of government had been deposed and the government he was leading was overthrown. I had to think for a while before responding but finally said, "No, I haven't been unseated; the wife still has a chair for me to sit in at home."

Chapter Ten

Learned Lessons of Life

In the process of developing this book and recounting all the humorous and comical occurrences throughout my life, I have compiled certain lessons and axioms learned through my experiences during each stage of my life. They are based on and follow in the same order as they appear in each preceding chapter of this book.

CHAPTER ONE

1. If, as a child, you are ever asked to carry a live chicken, cover it as best you can and choose the least populated route to reach your destination.
2. If you are dealing with poultry, make sure you know the difference between a goose and a turkey.
3. Pick your friends wisely, if you are entrusting them with fowl and money at the same time.
4. Beware of any co-delivery man who is delayed in delivering an order when the delivery is to a bar.

CHAPTER TWO

1. In running for any class election in high school, always pre-approve your campaign slogan.

2. If you are taught by nuns, always check out their footwear; never curse or use untoward language in their presence, and if you are of the male gender, never smoke while at a urinal.
3. In the event you are taking a test and looking at another student's answers, never add to his or her answer if that person's answer is "I don't know the answer."
4. If attending a high-school football game, never sit next to a person who has a flask of Jack Daniel's and has sons playing in the game.
5. If you are trying out for a high-school basketball team, at the tryout, do not attempt to pass the ball to the team's star player. Instead, discreetly try to stay in the back of the line, so you will be passing the ball to a less-experienced player.
6. If you are trying out for a high-school baseball team and are placed on the team as a reserve, be satisfied with sitting on the bench. If called upon, obey all steal signs given by the coach. Never think that avoiding them will allow you to succeed in stealing the base. Avoid all thoughts of "going out in a blaze of glory."

CHAPTER THREE

1. If working on a golf course and you are spraying the greens, always use an enhancer substance and not an eradicator substance.
2. If you are playing golf, make sure that the rest of your foursome are off the green.
3. If you have little or no experience driving a manual shift, don't drive a vehicle having one.

CHAPTER FOUR

1. If you are attending college and intend to witness a groundbreaking ceremony, always be on the lookout for loose ground and empty beer cans close to the site where the ceremony is being held.
2. When attending any athletic event, should a skirmish break out between the participating teams, try to get your friends to sing the national anthem in unison, in an attempt to stop the fighting.
3. Report to the police, any sighting of a suspicious person wearing a cassock and entering a liquor store.

CHAPTER FIVE

1. If you are in a moot court competition in law school, never choose a teammate who is catatonic.
2. When your car is not functioning properly, let the local auto center diagnose the problem rather than volunteering the name of an auto part that you think is at fault.

CHAPTER SIX

1. If you intend to enter the military and your last name begins with a "Z," go into court beforehand and have your name changed before enlisting.
2. Always divulge your full educational background to military personnel in order to receive fair treatment.
3. Buy two pairs of military dress shoes so you will never have to stand inspection with two right-footed shoes.

4. Never borrow another soldier's clothing unless he has a name that is short and easy to pronounce and you know every detail about his hometown.
5. Before going into the service, either have your chest hair shaved or wear a regular T-shirt, not a V-necked one.

CHAPTER SEVEN

As an Attorney:

1. If there are more than three attorneys in the building that houses your law office, be sure to highlight your name with a red, blinking, neon arrow on the front façade of the building listing each attorney's name.
2. Be sure to check the spring on your attorney chair in your office or have a safe, soft, and smooth landing spot in case it malfunctions.
3. Make sure you address the jury you have picked properly: no Women-Gentlemen of the jury; no Men-Ladies of the jury.
4. If you recognize a person in the jury pool, but can't remember how you know him or her, use a preemptory challenge rather than questioning him or her to establish cause.
5. In an assault case, try to have a football or rugby coach on your jury.
6. Never, ever allow your ex-wife's best friend on the jury that is hearing your client's case.
7. When any client in prison mentions "swan dive," immediately call the warden.

8. In a driving under the influence case, never try the bath-in-rubbing-alcohol defense.
9. In a guilty plea proceeding, if the Judge asks your client, "Are you satisfied with the services that your attorney has performed?" Tell your client the question requires a yes or no answer.
10. When representing a defendant in prison, always ask him before the guilty plea if he would rather stay in prison or be released.
11. In representing any defendant who is incarcerated, check beforehand to verify that he does not have a twin in prison and that he does not have the same, identical name as another prisoner.
12. Advise any defendant charged with burglary, where during the burglary he provides his real name to the victim-homeowner, that it will be tough sledding for him to be found not guilty.
13. If appointed standby counsel, you can advise the defendant as to what he should say, but do not advise him what he should call the district attorney.
14. In any domestic relations case involving a child needing braces, have the insistent parent scanned for any dental impressions on their person, prior to the conference.
15. In any domestic relations case, where at the conference the parties become heated in their exchanges and appear to be on the brink of losing it, be sure that there is a deputy sheriff nearby, not in the men's or ladies' room.
16. In any deposition where an ex-wife has in the past decimated their forest-like backyard, never ask the ex-husband if he lives on a wooded lot.

17. In a prostitution case, suggest to the Judge that the appropriate sentence to be imposed is one in which the defendant is ordered to leave town by sundown and given a one-way bus ticket to a distant destination.

18. In any open lewdness case where your client leaps into a sticker bush in order to avoid detection, suggest to the Judge that the ensuing pain was sufficient punishment.

19. In any mental-health proceeding, before the hearing, ask the nurse the meaning of "shark." Always take an umbrella with you on a rainy day, and make sure you watch the weather report, especially the wind direction and wind velocity, before leaving for the hearing.

20. When told by a client that you are not wanted as the attorney and are ordered to say nothing, never accept blame for the outcome of the case.

21. In a retail theft, always advise a client that committing a second offense in order to garner money to pay off fines and costs from the first offense will never fly as a defense of justification.

22. Advise a client that entering a store near closing time, and sleeping until the store is closed with the intention of stealing, is not only illegal but also can be dangerous to one's health and well-being.

23. Advise a client that attempting to put on four pairs of jeans and then leave a store without paying is not only illegal but also will not gain him entry into the *Guinness World Records*.

CHAPTER EIGHT

As a Magisterial District Judge:

1. When appointed or elected to office, have a large, illuminated sign with your name on it conspicuously above the front door entrance; never use a sign that has "vacant" on it, unless it is hung on the restroom door.

2. Never allow a dead guinea hen, bagged or not, to be brought into your courtroom.

3. In any case involving dog attacks on chickens, have ready and available on your bench an accurate egg productivity calculator.

4. In campaigning for office, while going door to door, avoid all homes that have large, growling dogs.

5. While going door to door, make sure to wear a sign that states, "Believe me, I am not selling anything" and another sign that states, "I am not the Verizon man."

6. If campaigning on a rainy day, don't take an umbrella with you, but if you do, avoid all walkways with trellises.

7. In preparing a campaign brochure, use a picture that is less than flattering. That technique will enhance your image when you do appear in person.

8. When on night duty, obliterate the word "sleep "entirely from your mind. Keep your pager at arm's length at all times and have a full supply of coffee nearby. When night duty is finally over, revive the concept of uninterrupted sleep, ditch the pager, and don't drink coffee for at least a month.

9. In performing a wedding ceremony, be wary of anyone responding to the statement, "If anyone present has an objection to the union of the two people now before me, speak now or forever hold your peace." If an objection is

raised by an adult person attending the wedding in the courtroom, be prepared to deal with the details of the objection, appropriately.

10. Never skip a line in the document containing the ceremonial words used to perform the wedding. If you do, you may give the bride and groom the impression that theirs is a union that should not be entered into soberly.

11. In the ring exchange portion of the wedding ceremony, be careful to instruct the bride-to-be to put the wedding ring on the groom-to-be's finger, with the words, "Receive this ring as a treasure that I will now give you" and not "Receive this ring with the pleasure I will now give you."

CHAPTER NINE

As a Retiree:

1. Retire your gavel gracefully and discreetly to a remote desk drawer, where it will be out of sight and out of mind. Do not entertain the notion that you are still the boss. Instead, resign yourself to the fact that decisions will now be made on a 50–50 basis with your wife at home and that half a loaf is better than no loaf at all. Delete from your vocabulary the words "objection sustained" and "objection overruled." Use the Bible to read rather than to swear in witnesses. Find a comfortable rocking chair for relaxation and to counter any reports that you have been unseated.

2. Settle into retirement gracefully and thankfully. Disregard any disparaging comments that imply that your senior status carries with it the connotation of graying hair, decreased wisdom, and ambulation. Enjoy the remaining years and all the joys and happiness that the past years have given you. Finally, remember that LIFE CAN'T BE ALL SERIOUS!

Made in the USA
Monee, IL
14 September 2026

63198310R00066